MI-BODY

A positive & interactive guide to help you improve your mental & physical health

Michael Parker

Contents

Prologue

"The secret of health for both mind and body is not to mourn for the past, not to worry about the future or to anticipate troubles, but to live the present moment wisely and earnestly."

I am writing this, as a 31-year-old married man (love you, Laura!) who like many others, I have struggled to cope with whatever pressures life has thrown my way. I have experienced phases of my life where I have consistently felt low and have developed a real understanding of the symptoms of depression, anxiety and other mental health issues. Members of my family have been diagnosed with mental illness and I have seen how these disorders can affect people in all walks of life.

This book shares a small part of my story whilst outlining the activities I have done in my personal life to improve my mental and physical health. You could also call it an average guy's guide to feeling better on the inside and out!

Introduction

"Self-identity", as defined in the Oxford Dictionary, is the perception or recognition of one's characteristics as a particular individual, especially in relation to social context.

As a kid and young adult, I was obsessed with sports. I played everything possible: basketball, rugby, cricket, football, volleyball, whatever was on after school or before school started, I was there. My identity growing up was Michael the sportsman, the teammate, the guy who was always either throwing, hitting, kicking, passing, dribbling or shooting a ball. I loved the competition, the structure it gave my life with training and games on set days and most of all my teammates. There is nothing like setting your teammate up to score, having their back in a tackle, the high fives, hugs—team sports are the best!

As a 17-year-old I decided to focus directly on basketball. I had always been very tall, and basketball came naturally to me at school. Upon signing with Doncaster Danum Eagles in the National Basketball League, I found out a few of the players had earned American college scholarships and as soon as I heard that this could be a possibility, I wanted to do everything in my power to achieve this. I moved to Doncaster and lived there for a year so I could use the facilities and train with the team every day. I developed myself as a player and I hit the gym hard to build muscle and fill out my lanky frame. By the end of the year, I was a six-foot-five, 16-stone athlete ready to compete with players from America for scholarship places.

I had booked a trip to Florida to have trials at a few colleges over there. The week before I was due to fly, my coach wanted to make a video of me and another player who had the same aspirations. A lot of players have a mixtape as such to help with their profile and the hope was, that this could have done the same for me. Forty minutes into the gameplay and recording I went to lay the ball into the basket and took some contact from the defender to do so. I landed on my right foot and it just buckled. Pop. Crack. My foot was facing the wrong way. I had dislocated and broken my ankle in three parts.

The trip was cancelled and surgery was scheduled to realign, pin, plate and wire my bones back together. I laid in the hospital bed the following week heartbroken, unable to sleep, thinking I should have been boarding the plane at the airport.

I finally got discharged to come home from the hospital after what had seemed like the longest ten days of my life. After finishing my course of warfarin injections into my stomach and getting the go-ahead to move around I was determined to make things right. I decided to take a chair outside and shoot some hoops. Even though I had a broken ankle I could still do drills sat down and I spent the next six weeks doing whatever I could to get better as a player and athlete. I stayed positive and as soon as my cast was cut off I threw myself into the long, winding road of rehabilitation. The following springtime, 12 months after surgery I rebooked my trip to the States.

Getting in touch with American colleges about scholarships as an overseas player is like any job application, you can compose the "perfect" email and send it to several college coaches but a lot of the time you never hear anything back.

This left me with one shot at a college in Lake Wales, Florida.

As I walked into the reception at Warner University I was greeted by the head coach who had previously worked with over 30 NBA players as college athletes, helping all-time greats like Chris Paul and Kevin Durant prepare for the NBA draft. A short tour of the 300 acre campus followed, concluding at the basketball court. Trial time. After seeing the state of the art facilities and meeting a number of friendly university staff along the way, I knew this was the right place for me and my nerves kicked in knowing what was resting on the next hour or so. The coach put me through a number of shooting, dribbling, rebounding, defensive and athletic drills to test my game and my ability, he then finished the trial with post moves and 20 shots-18 feet away from the basket. I made the last 5 in a row to give me a very respectable 17 out of 20. A high five was exchanged and we sat on the bleachers to discuss the trial.

After briefly discussing our backgrounds, clearing up that not all British people like tea and my goals both athletically and academically, I got the feedback I had wanted for so long. "That went really well, we would love to have you with us." The coach detailed what I did well and areas where I could develop. He explained that due to the time of year, most of his roster spots had been filled already. He could only offer me a part scholarship with additional incentives when I got into the top 10 playing rotation and starting line-up.

He then told me more about the program: about his support staff which included an assistant coach, a strength & conditioning coach with professional athletic experience, two certified athletic trainers, a gameday operations team, two team doctors, two sports information directors and several other team managers and counsellors. He mentioned the competition and that every year Warner had the opportunity to play the very best NCAA (National Collegiate Athletic Association) division 1 teams, having played against Butler Bulldogs and were scheduled to play Florida Gators (who a few years earlier had won back to back National titles meaning they were the best college team in the whole of America). He also spoke about his professional relationships for when I graduated and how he had helped place players in professional leagues and programs around the world from the NBA D League (now G League) to England, France, Germany, Switzerland, Puerto Rico, The Dominican, Argentina, Indonesia and Canada. I was amazed, I had finally got the chance to live my American dream.

I left Florida later that week armed with Warner Royals t-shirts & merchandise, a school brochure and financial & enrolment paperwork for international students. For the prior two years I had lived very frugally, spending on average, less than £30 a week and banking every pay packet I worked for. Even with this big effort, the part scholarship or decent exchange rate, I couldn't afford the remaining tuition and board fees so I was relying on other grants and student loans to make up the difference. I applied for a student loan and was rejected and even wrote to my local MP to see if there was any way around student loans only being available to students going to university in the UK. No luck.

My dream was shattered for the 2nd time in two years.

Later that summer I understood that my goal of playing college ball in America was over, so I signed to play for Bradford Dragons in England's National Basketball league to continue my basketball education and hopefully prime myself for the next level.

After several Division 1 games, we were starting to hit our stride and on the weekend of my 21st birthday, we had back-to-back games on the Saturday and Sunday. After playing both games and getting home I couldn't walk up the stairs, I was in agony. I had just turned 21 but I looked like a 90-year-old trying to climb the staircase.

The years of wear and tear from sport and multiple injuries to my joints and body had caught up with me. I knew it was coming, but as this moment was approaching I kept looking the other way. I kept doing everything I could just to be "fit" for the Saturday games, I loved the game and I didn't want to let my teammates down.

My identity changed that weekend, knowing I couldn't keep up with the rigours of high level sport, I took some time away from the game to have treatments to try and repair my body. I never made it back. Sunday 13th November 2011 was my last ever game. My basketball career had ended way too early. I never quite made it to the professional ranks and will never know if I had what it takes… I understand how professional sportsmen and women struggle with adjusting to "retired" life. Even though I was not a professional I did train like one and I had the mentality of one. Weights five or six times a week, individual development sessions at home working on ball handling and shooting, trips to the park to work on agility and vertical jump ability, team training sessions and games in between work and coaching basketball in schools. When that has been your life and it gets taken away, you really feel like a wasted athlete. I have been down so many times over not being able to play and never knowing where the sport could have taken me.

I became just Michael. Lost. No identity, no career, and I really struggled mentally to find purpose with my life in order to move on to my next chapter.

"It's not an ending. It's just the point in the story where you turn the page."

Writing this nearly 10 years on from that weekend, I have accepted that my sporting years were a success rather than a what-could-have-been. For a while, I used to resent basketball for how it left me physically and mentally but now my love for the game is back with a bang. The lessons I learned from playing sports have helped me immensely in everyday life. Sport taught me how to stay disciplined, it developed my mental strength and installed a resilience in me to perform under pressure and to persevere through the challenges of life. It built my confidence and character and my "win together, lose together and never leave a teammate behind" mentality has earned me great respect from friends, family members and work colleagues.

I am no longer looking to develop myself to be the best sportsman. That drive, however, has not burned out and I now try to develop myself to be the best man I can be and a big part of that includes helping others when they need it.

Inspired by many great influences and teachers, I have collated my tips and ideas of activities you can do to improve your mental and physical health. You might continue reading and think "Cold showers? Phone box? Not a chance!" I wouldn't judge you either, at times I thought the same before trying these different things for the first time. I must say though that everything I have wrote on the following pages has helped make me feel better about myself. So, as you read on, I urge you to please try to have an open mind and think "I'll give that a go!"

I really hope you enjoy reading and remember… have a go, what's the worst that could happen?

Positive mindset

I am a big believer in the idea that being positive helps anyone's fight against mental illness. If you are going to a job that you dislike on a Monday, instead of saying, "Oh great, it's Monday, five days till the weekend." Try to be positive about the start of the week, "It's Monday, let's have a great day!" Having this approach will instantly make you feel better.

Another situation I have noticed in everyday life is that when you ask people if they have had a good day, some people will say, "Not bad." I fell into this group of people myself, but in an attempt to be more positive I have changed the way I respond to questions like this by substituting "Not bad" with "Very good, thank you!"

Having a positive mindset is important in helping you fight mental health issues. Optimism and positive thinking can also help prevent some health conditions from starting in the first place. Other ways to promote a positive mindset include:

Starting your day with a positive statement. Have you ever gotten up late, got stuck in traffic on the way to work and then felt that nothing good happened for the rest of the day? This is probably because you started the day with a negative experience and that negative emotion continued throughout the day. Instead of letting this take hold of you, try to start with a positive affirmation. Talk to yourself in front of the mirror when you're getting ready and say phrases like "Today will be a good day!" You might feel stupid but say them out loud and proud! You will be amazed to see how much your day improves.

Surrounding yourself with positive people. When you are around positive people, their positivity will rub off on you. You will hear positive outlooks on life, positive stories and phrases. This will affect your own line of thinking. It can sometimes be difficult to surround yourself with good influences so you may also want to watch videos of motivational people and speakers who radiate positivity. You can also listen to upbeat songs to give you a boost. One just came on as I was writing this! Imagine Dragons—"On Top of the World".

Focus on the good things, however small they seem. Let's face it, there is no such thing as the perfect day or perfect life. Something has to go wrong along the way. So, when these bad things happen, always try to think of the silver lining. For example, if you get stuck in traffic on your way to work think about how you can finish listening to your favourite album or finish another episode of a podcast you have been listening to.

Find humour in bad situations. Always use humour even if it is in the most impossible situations or darkest times of your life. Think about how this may turn into a funny story one day for your family and friends.

Turn mistakes into lessons. No one is perfect. Everyone makes mistakes whether they happen at work or in your home life. Instead of thinking too much about your mistakes, turn them into lessons for next time and in turn, you will motivate yourself instead of dwelling on your negative thoughts.

Finally, finish each day with positive thoughts. Every night before you go to sleep, think about the best things that happened that day and choose a top 3. Laura told me about this, and she does this all the time. She sleeps like a baby!

Phone box

"Twenty years ago, the internet was an escape from the real world. Today the real world is an escape from the internet."

Social media platforms such as Facebook and Instagram are brilliant for keeping in touch with friends and family. I love tagging my friends in a funny video on Facebook or showing them some amazing scenery on Instagram to help them plan their next holiday!

Social networks can however have a negative effect on people too. You can see people you went to school with, old work colleagues, influencers and celebrities and it is easy to start comparing your life to theirs. Social media doesn't always show the grind that people go through to do amazing things. In many ways it is just a highlight reel of people looking their best or having the best time.

These platforms can make a lot of people feel like they are not handsome or pretty enough if they don't get enough likes or followers. Too much scrolling through feeds or posts can pick apart your self-esteem and mental health. With every scroll of the mouse or tap at the screen thoughts like "I wish that was me" or "I wish I was there" can come into your mind. You start to think about the things that you don't have, instead of being grateful for the things you do have.

As I said, there are some brilliant aspects of social media so I do use the platforms, however, I noticed that they were taking up too much time in my life. After finishing work and having my evening meal I could just waste the night away by scrolling on Facebook or Instagram for hours and it didn't make me feel good. I might have got the odd laugh at a video or seen something amazing but on the whole, it just felt like a waste of my time.

A good tip to start limiting your screen time would be to turn off notifications for social media apps. You seem to get bombarded with sounds, badges and banners from these apps and when you go to view your notifications, Facebook is telling you about a person's birthday who you have met once in your life and have not spoken to in 10 years. Once you're on the app, the scrolling starts…

I also have an imaginary phone box for my phone during the evening. I might have 30 minutes after dinner to catch up on messages, emails or anything else but then I place my phone into the "phone box" in order to look after my psychological health. By doing this I have noticed a decrease in the times that I've had low self-esteem and anxiety. I am also much more productive during these periods!

My "phone box" is at the end of the sofa, the screen faces down into the fabric and my data is switched off, so I don't get distracted. Apart from taking the occasional phone call or replying to messages, I try to stay off my phone as much as possible during the evening.

Your "phone box" can be anything. Another room, the biscuit tin, a cupboard in your kitchen. You could even buy a special box if you really wanted! Anything encourages you to live in the real world rather than on social media.

Nature

"In nature nothing is perfect, and everything is perfect. Trees can be contorted, bent in weird ways and they're still beautiful."

People are the same, we are all different, but everyone is beautiful in their own way. Being in nature, or even viewing scenes of nature on the TV (your cue to add a few David Attenborough TV shows to your Netflix list) can reduce anger and fear and increase pleasant feelings. Sitting down or lying in green spaces not only makes you feel better emotionally but also contributes to your physical wellbeing by reducing your blood pressure and heart rate, easing muscle tension and stopping or slowing the production of stress hormones.

There is a technique called "grounding" or "earthing" which means to have direct contact with the earth's surface by standing or walking barefoot on grass, sand etc. The earth transfers energy from the ground into your body which can increase your overall health. Research has shown that barefoot contact with the earth can produce nearly instant changes in a variety of physiological measures, helping to improve sleep, reduce pain, decrease muscle tension and lower stress. In the summer months, I add barefoot yoga to my weekly routine. Doing yoga barefoot on grass or sand will give you a boost both physically and mentally. So, next time you are in a park, football field or another green space on a nice dry day, kick off your shoes, take your socks off and give it a try!

Spending time in nature will also tick off a few of your

mental health needs such as:

Exercise: A lot of people live in man-made estates in towns or city centres, meaning unless you live near a park or in the countryside and have forests on your doorstep (or other features and products of the earth) you will have to travel to spend time in nature. Once you are there, you will want to explore, this will mean either getting on a bike, swimming or hiking. Hiking offers a nearly instant feeling of peace and contentment while significantly decreasing negative and obsessive thoughts. Spending an hour and a half or so walking in a natural environment also gets your heart rate up and works the muscles in your body.

Strong body = strong mind = strong spirit

Sunlight: Being in the great outdoors also increases your opportunities to benefit from sunlight. Sunlight is a free mood enhancer as it increases the levels of serotonin in the brain. Now you know why most people are happier in the summertime! Don't forget the sun cream!

Fresh air: Fresh air helps to send oxygen through the blood and allows your lungs to work at full capacity which equals more brainpower and better mental health.

In summary, being outside in nature can do wonders for relieving anxiety, stress and mild to moderate depression. Nature boosts endorphin levels and dopamine production, which promotes happiness.

So, why not take a walk in the woods? You will come out feeling taller than the trees.

Inner child

Adulthood is amazing, the first time in your life where you have the freedom to do what you want, when you want, with no parents telling you what to do (my mum still tries, bless her!). Independence creates opportunities, and like many people in their early adult life I have been able to see plenty of new places and experience new things which I just couldn't do when I was a kid.

This new independence can however bring pressure. We are now on our own two feet financially and with the choices we make. These newfound pressures can convey mental health problems and worries. With this in mind, I always try to be a child at heart, it takes me back to the times when I didn't have many worries. When I was a kid, I enjoyed the small things and was happy with almost anything. Your inner child is a part of your mind that still retains its innocence, creativity, awe and wonder towards life so having this mentality of tapping into your inner child in adult life is invaluable.

To connect to your inner child, I would recommend you write a list of things that made you happy when you were younger and then chase down those activities or places.

During the Covid-19 pandemic the big events in our lives were cancelled or couldn't be done; no meals out, no nights out, no stag and hen parties, no weddings and holidays cancelled.

With a heavily impacted social life, there was a perfect chance to reincarnate 11-year-old Michael! During the months of the pandemic, five things from my childhood really took centre stage and helped me through it mentally. The activities were as follows, hopefully, you can relate:

1- Mario Kart 64: I played this for hours with my sister when I was younger, it was such a fun game to play. We used to try to make sure we were both on the podium but most of the time we would try to blow each other up with the turtle shells as we found this more entertaining! Playing this game again brought some serious nostalgia and it also amazed me how we ever played on a 14-inch TV!

2- Shooting hoops: Every day after school I used to rush home to go outside the house and practice my basketball skills till my dad pulled his Volvo onto the drive when he finished work. In the summer I could be out till 9pm–10pm as I loved it so much. Going up to the court during the pandemic was not to develop myself anymore, it was just to have fun and the sound of the swoosh through the net is just so soothing, you can't beat it!

3- Park and garden games: A garden shed should have the following items as a minimum: bowls set with a jack, frisbee, and a bat and ball. I lost count of the number of times we threw the frisbee over the summer months. A hundred catches in a row are no problem for us!

4- Monopoly: Whose childhood didn't have a story of playing monopoly with the family until one of you got so annoyed that the board got flipped! Board games are so good to bring back childhood memories and they also give you a break from screen time.

5- Bike rides: This really brings me back to my childhood; weekend rides with my dad and sister when my mum was at work stand out. One of the main things that helped me reminisce was that I was using the same "push iron" that I rode on when I was younger! The Saracen bike got a refurb at the local Halfords bike servicing centre and I even used it to go to the supermarket for supplies! Those trips to the supermarket on the bike really brought out a sense of adventure!

"We don't stop playing because we grow old; we grow old because we stop playing."

Time to create your childhood activity list.

Creating a list

Without a doubt having a to-do list or schedule for your day can create a sense of inner mastery. When you are down or struggling it is hard to find your purpose or a sense of achievement. When you tick off a task on your to-do list you get a visual moment of success and an invisible pat on the back. This really helps when looking back on your day as you can see how much you have achieved. Let's face it, most days you won't have big moments, that's what makes the big holidays, weddings and other key life events so special. So, on the quiet days, it is still good to look back and think, "You know what, today has been great. Look what I have managed to get done."

It is important to not overwhelm yourself with the amount of tasks you need to complete. You should choose an achievable number of tasks to accomplish, so choosing maybe four to five tasks a day is enough and you can have different lists for different categories for example: "self-care", "jobs for the house" and "work to do". To get started my recommendation would be to create a task list for self-care and include things like:

- Go for a run or exercise.
- 20 minutes of yoga or stretches.
- Write in my journal about three good things from today.
- Get some sunlight and fresh air.

Creating a list is the not so well-kept secret of becoming productive. Mental health waivers when we don't have a purpose or something to accomplish, so make sure you have a list that will help you stay motivated to keep taking care of your thoughts and body.

	Exercise	Yoga	Journal	Fresh air
Monday	✓	✓	✓	✓
Tuesday	✓	✓	✓	✓
Wednesday	✓	✓	✓	✓
Thursday	✓	✓	✓	✓
Friday	✓	✓	✓	✓
Saturday	✓	✓	✓	✓
Sunday	✓	✓	✓	✓

Laughing

"A day without laughter is a day wasted."

"Laughter is the best medicine."

"A good laugh heals a lot of hurts."

There is a reason there are so many quotes about laughter being positive. Laughter triggers the release of endorphins, the body's natural feel-good chemicals. Endorphins promote an overall sense of well-being and can even temporarily relieve pain. Laughter also decreases stress hormones and increases immune cells and infection-fighting antibodies, thus improving your resistance to disease.

There are many things you can do to have a laugh. After a busy, maybe stressful day at work put a comedy sketch or comedy show on TV. My personal favourite comedians include (in no particular order) Peter Kay, Paddy McGuiness, Kevin Hart, Gary Delaney, Jack Whitehall, Michael McIntyre, Rob Beckett, Romesh Ranganathan, Joel Dommett, Ricky Gervais and Rhod Gilbert.

Tickling is also a great activity to do to make you laugh. Plan a "tickle session" with your partner and get them to tickle you from head to toe. The feeling you get after this is brilliant due to the laughing fit you will have just had!

Make it your intention to laugh and smile more. Ensure it becomes part of your day-to-day. Follow someone funny on social media. Read jokes and don't be afraid to tell jokes! You will probably get a laugh even if the joke isn't funny!

I'm not quite qualified to tell "dad jokes" just yet, however here are a few of my personal favourites to get you started:

My pet mouse Elvis died the other day. He got caught in a trap.

Why don't eggs tell jokes? They'd crack each other up.

Did you hear the rumour about butter? Well, I'm not going to spread it!

Why couldn't the bicycle stand up by itself? It was two tired.

What time did the man go to the dentist? Tooth hurty.

How many tickles does it take to make an octopus laugh? Ten tickles.

How do celebrities stay cool? They have many fans.

What do you call it when Batman skips church? Christian Bale.

How do you organise a space party? You planet.

Dancing

My first night out was as a shy, awkward, 18-year-old who didn't drink alcohol, what could go right? It was a nervous night out from what I can remember. The night started slowly and after midnight we made our way to the nightclub in Shakey Wakey (Wakefield).

The music was blaring, and everyone was having a great time. I was still a little reserved but after seeing the rest of the club goers let themselves loose, I felt finally ready. I started to dance... well if you can call it that! I had a great time and felt euphoric and so positive when the night came to an end.

I wanted to write this chapter after a recent wedding I went to. The bride and groom had a live saxophonist to go along with the Motown, funk and dance tunes that were being played by the DJ. I felt like I was in Café Mambo, Ibiza. My moves are now more polished... in my opinion! However, the feeling I get when dancing has stayed the same. I think dancing is one of the best things you can do for your mental health. Complete novices like myself can take part, whether it's at a nightclub, a wedding, your own home, with a partner or just on your own - I have been guilty of throwing a few shapes about in the shower from time to time! It makes you laugh seeing others dance, it burns calories and rhythmic movement has been shown to trigger the release of endorphins in your brain, which can boost your mood.

Overall, dancing is a fun way to exercise and when you start to move your feet and hips, your brain quietens down and any stress or worries you have start to take a back seat. The mental escape it offers is invaluable and will give your mind a chance to recharge itself.

If you're nervous or lacking in confidence to give dancing a go, just remember I was that person too at 18-years-old. Be yourself. Pretend like no one's watching. Act confident until you feel it and one day you may end up buying an online dance masterclass to learn your own wedding dance like yours truly!

So, what are you waiting for? Time to dust off those dancing shoes!

Water in motion

Water in motion produces negative ions, which are known to relieve stress, reduce tension, fight depression and increase energy. In short, all these negative ions produce some real positive vibes!

There is a reason that your stereotypical Australian or Californian surfer dudes and dudettes are so laid back, fun-loving and happy. They spend hours at the beach, in the sea, chasing the waves. It's not just "riding the wave" that puts a smile on their faces, it's the negative ions the waves are producing that increase the flow of oxygen to their brains. This makes them more alert, less drowsy, and it increases their mental energy. It's a bit of a generalisation, sure, but surfers seem to be the happiest people in the world and the science is there to back this up.

Water in motion comes in many forms. Waves for one are inspiring in their own way, not because they rise and fall, but because each time they fall they never fail to rise again. This is such an important message with mental health, you will have your ups and downs but always rise again!

Other forms of water which break apart air molecules when moving to produce negative ions include rivers, waterfalls and even water fountains! My neighbours have a water fountain in their garden, and it is situated maybe 10 metres away from my bedroom window meaning I get a double boost! When I'm outside I get the feel-good vibe from the negative ions and when I'm going to sleep, I hear the tranquil noise of running water which helps me to relax and drop into a meditative state.

Water in motion is normally quite picturesque, the waves at the beach, a plunge waterfall, it's normally something that catches your eye. Rain showers however are not something we associate with positive thoughts. After all, sunny days are so special because of the rain. Rain showers do produce negative ions though, so next time rain is forecasted don't sigh, plan to play in the rain for better mental health or put your running trainers on. There have been multiple times I've ran in the rain and once I've got over the fact that I'm getting soaked, I have really enjoyed being outside!

Always choose positivity, apart from ions. There is nothing negative or unhealthy about negative ions which water in motion produces.

Time for your next trip to the seaside!

Cold showers

Let's start where we left off, water in motion. In this case, cold showers! After reading about cold showers online and exploring the benefits of having cold showers I decided to make them a fixture in my everyday life. So, Monday to Friday it's cold showers all the way. I still enjoy a warm shower (who doesn't?) but I now save these as a treat at a weekend. It is so important to have balance in your life, having these little rewards after a period of excellence and discipline will keep you motivated and can help you to create good habits.

Cold showers offer many benefits to the body and can help improve health in numerous ways, from relaxing the mind to improving your skin's condition and enhancing blood flow.

From my research, here are 10 reasons why you should give cold showers a go:

1. Promotes fat loss
Simply pouring ice-cold water onto your body can help you to lose weight. Cold showers activate brown fat, which generates heat around the body.

The increased activity of the "good fat" burns calories to keep the body warm. Research shows that cold temperatures can boost brown fat by 15 times higher than the normal amount.

2. Improves immunity

Regular cold showers can trigger an increase in the metabolic speed rate and the number of white blood cells in the body, which then help fight diseases.

3. They enhance blood circulation

Improved circulation means better overall cardiovascular health. Among the many benefits of taking cold showers is having a good blood flow. It allows the blood to rush down to the organs to stay warm.

4. Drains lymphatic system

Cold showers help boost the activity of the lymphatic system, which works to carry out waste from cells. This then reduces the risk of infections.

5. Promotes emotional resilience

Cold showers can help develop a nervous system that is resilient to stress. The effort alone serves as a small form of oxidative stress, which the body would adapt over time and teach the brain to prepare for stress.

6. Lowers stress

As the brain learns how to deal with stressful situations, cold showers could also help cut the levels of uric acid and boost glutathione in the blood, which helps reduce stress.

7. Lowers chances of depression

Cold showers have been found to relieve symptoms of depression by stimulating what is called "the blue spot" on the brain that releases noradrenaline, a chemical that plays a role in alleviating depression.

8. Increases testosterone levels

For men, heat or warm showers can affect the DNA, RNA and protein synthesis in the testes. There has been a study on rats that showed that having 15 minutes of increased heat on their testes led to a significant decrease in testosterone. This suggests that cold temperatures could reverse this effect.

9. Promotes faster muscle recovery

There is a reason full-time athletes use ice baths or cryotherapy chambers (an extreme cold chamber that either uses liquid nitrogen or refrigerated cold air to expose individuals to temperatures below −100 °C). These treatments after intense training improve circulation and help remove some lactic acid, which can speed up the body's recovery. Cold showers have a similar effect on the body.

10. Enhances skin and hair

The benefits of taking a cold shower not only give better health, but they can also make people look better. Ice-cold water can help reduce the risk of losing too many natural oils from the skin and hair. The cold water also helps make the hair appear shiny and strengthens its grip on the scalp.

Brace yourself, the first one will be a big shock to your system, and you may want to start with the hot tap flowing to ease yourself in. When ready, turn on the cold and try to bare it for 30 seconds. Once you're up to having 4-minute cold showers five times a week you might want to check out Wim "The Iceman" Hof for your next cold challenge!

Deep breathing

Inhale through the nose, exhale through the mouth, inhale, exhale, inhale, exhale… relax.

Deep breathing is a practice that allows more air to flow into your body and it can help you relax. When you concentrate on your breathing you can help your body and mind to rest. It can calm your nerves, and reduce stress and anxiety. Enabling you to have a calm and grounded well-being.

To begin, relax your eyelids and take a gentle full inhale through your nose and when you let it out, purse your lips together and steadily let the air out as if you're blowing bubbles into a drink through a straw. Continue for a few minutes and develop your rhythm. After a few minutes add in a meditation exercise on the in and out-breath to help steady and balance the mind. On the next inhale silently repeat the phrase "I calm the body." On the next exhale say the same for the mind, "I calm the mind." Repeat this for a few minutes. After 5 minutes of deep breathing, you will suddenly feel calmer.

An alternative exercise to the above to also lower your heart rate and improve your focus is alternate nostril breathing. A quick 2 minutes of the following should do the trick:

1. Close your right nostril with your right thumb and breathe in fully through your left nostril.

2. Close your left nostril with your finger (note, that both nostrils will now be closed).

3. Open your right nostril and breathe out.

4. Breathe in through your right nostril.

5. Close your right nostril with your thumb (note, that both nostrils will now be closed).

6. Open your left nostril and breathe out.

7. Repeat for 2 minutes.

The type of deep breathing you practice will differ depending on your circumstances. Based on experience, here are my three rules to remember:

-   If you are struggling **to relax**, breathe out for longer than you breathe in. Try counting to 4 on your inhale and to 7 on the exhale to relax and rest your body.

-   If you need **more energy**, breathe in for longer than you breathe out. Inhale for a count of 5 and exhale for a count of 2.

-   If you want to **increase your focus**, try box breathing. 4 count inhale, 4 count hold, 4 count exhale, 4 count hold.

Sleep

We can all relate to feeling tired, lethargic and run down if we don't get enough sleep. The recommended amount of sleep needed for a grown adult is around 8 hours a night (some people need more, some need less). A lot of people are unable to get their recommended amount of sleep for several reasons: a new-born baby, stress, bringing work home and other worries that you may have which can keep you up at night. If you fail to get enough sleep over a number of nights or a longer period of time, then it can take its toll on your body and your mental health. Lack of sleep can eventually cause hallucinations, anger outbursts, mood swings and can also lead to an inability to concentrate which truly impacts your work and personal life. In short, having enough sleep is a big factor in your physical and mental health.

Approximately, 1 in 3 people in the UK suffer from poor sleep, including myself. I wish I was someone who could just close their eyes in the car, on a plane or the train and just fall off to sleep, however that will never be me.

Since adulthood hit me properly, I have had some terrible nights. I could be wide awake at 5am after having no sleep, looking at the alarm waiting for it to go off an hour or so later and when it did, I would be in a bad mood straight away to start my day. Most of the time I couldn't sleep because I was worried about my career. As a 21-year-old, I had just retired from basketball due to injuries and my basketball coaching job had stopped due to a funding freeze with the council. I was left with 21 hours a week working at an independent petrol station with no career prospects.

I would apply for hundreds of jobs and would get 20 unsuccessful emails back and never hear from the rest. This worry kept me up at night with questions like how can I buy a house, go on holiday and eventually support a family? I needed to reset and try and tackle the problem head-on as I could see the draining effect sleep deprivation was having on me mentally and physically.

The quality of my sleep has got a lot better over the years, I have tried a number of techniques that help me to relax and switch off. I don't worry too much about my career and life in general anymore but from time to time there are things in life we can't escape from, and these things can affect our capacity to switch our minds off at night.

I have tried many things to help me beat insomnia like wearing a mask and earplugs (sometimes if you look the part, you feel the part!). I have been gifted deep sleep pillow sprays and gels which have worked from time to time. The scent is very strong so after a couple of sprays your mind seems to forget what it was concentrating on and you focus on the smell. I've focused on breathing techniques, breathing in for a count of 7 and out for a count of 11 to benefit from its calming effect. I've listened to sounds of water trickling or raindrops falling, counted backwards from 1,000, recapped the events of my day and even tried guided sleep meditation where a man or woman with a very soothing voice speaks to you as you try to drift off… "10, relax your shoulders into your mattress and neck and head into your pillow as you prepare for the deepest sleep you have ever had. 9, let all the tension drain out of your legs and ankles… you are about to fall into a deep sleep." You get the idea.

I recently added a beginner's yoga pose into my night-time routine. I get washed, brush my teeth and then proceed to get in the legs-up-the-wall pose or for you yogis out there the Viparita Karani. Keeping my legs straight against the wall whilst sinking my back into the carpet, I hold this pose for 3 minutes every night whilst closing my eyes and switching off my mind. Unlike many yoga poses this hold is not stressful or taxing on your muscles, it is completely the opposite: relaxing and refreshing. The legs-up-the-wall pose also gives blood circulation a gentle boost towards my upper body and head, which creates a pleasant rebalancing after a day of standing or sitting for a long time. As soon as the 3-minute timer buzzes I make my way to my bed. My legs and ankles feel lighter and less swollen due to the blood flowing to my lower belly and my mind is relaxed and ready to follow my next and favourite deep sleep meditation exercise.

One of my best tips for falling asleep (excluding listening to Matthew McConaughey's calming tones reading you a bedtime story) is to follow a military technique that is reportedly used by the US army. It may take over 6 weeks to perfect, but it has made a huge difference to my now occasional struggles.

Here's how you do it:

1. Relax the muscles in your face, including the tongue, jaw and the muscles around the eyes.

2. Drop your shoulders as far down as they'll go, followed by your upper and lower arm, one side at a time.

3. Breathe out, relaxing your chest followed by your legs, starting from the thighs and working down.

4. You should then spend 10 seconds trying to clear your mind before thinking about one of the following images:

- You're lying in a canoe on a calm lake with nothing but a clear blue sky above you.

- You're lying in a black velvet hammock in a pitch-black room.

Good night, sleep tight, see you in the morning light!

Reading

As we hit the halfway point in terms of the number of chapters in this book and you have probably been reading for an hour or so* I want to ask you, how do you feel right now?

Pretty calm and relaxed, right? Reading puts our minds into a state similar to meditation as it helps us to achieve a mentally clear and emotionally calm and stable state. The activity has also been shown to help people sleep better and for the frequent lifetime reader, scanning the pages helps to keep good brain health in old age.

Reading offers a mental diversion from any unpleasant aspects of life. If you are having a bad day, the escapism reading offers you will allow your mind to wander and your imagination will take centre stage rather than your worries.

I used to think that reading was just an activity you do on holiday when lying on a sun lounger in between listening to music and eating. However, after making a new year's resolution to myself, I thought I would give reading a good go to increase my knowledge, expand my vocabulary and for the mental stimulation that it provides. I bought a few books, got comfy on the bean bag while the rain poured outside and hit the chapters.

Let's just say I have not looked back; television is great but there should always be room for a book in everyone's life.

"Reading to the mind is what exercise is to the body."

*Hopefully you have binge-read the book! If not, I apologise, please keep slogging away! I know I'm no J.K. Rowling!

Foam rolling

Foam rolling is a self-massage technique that uses a rubber cylinder to massage muscles in your body when you lay down on the roller and slowly move up and down.

I'm not going to lie to you and say this is an experience you will really enjoy. This is no hot stone massage or similar, foam rolling is more like a sports massage done by a very strong masseuse! The action of rolling on a foam roller can be quite a painful one, especially if you are trying to massage your outer quad or IT band and you weigh in around 16 stones (101.6kg) like someone I know!

However, massage (including self-myofascial release) does have several benefits for you. Just like stretching, foam rolling can be integral to injury prevention, increasing blood flow, decreasing soft-tissue density and relaxing tight muscles. By easing pain and stiffness, it may also help reduce levels of stress-related hormones in the body like cortisol.

As most people don't have the money to have a daily massage to ease their muscles and help them relax, your next best bet for "rolling away" the tension in your muscles is to buy a foam roller and spend 10 minutes on it a day after a workout or sitting at work.

My favourite muscle group to work with a foam roller is my back, in particular my upper back. As I sit at work all day on a laptop, I tend to bend my upper back so I can see the screen clearer. This bad habit has had some detrimental effects on my posture to the point where if I try to sit up straight it doesn't feel natural. This has meant I have developed poor spine mobility and increased tension in the surrounding muscles.

When I foam roll, I can feel the built-up tension in my muscles releasing and I also sometimes hear my back crack which to me is very satisfying (I love watching chiropractor visits online) as I know I am relieving pressure in my spine and in turn, I'm doing the best to look after my body and mind.

Have a go, what's the worst that could happen?

Stretching

Having played a lot of sports over the years, stretching, warming up and cooling down have always been very important for my body. Nowadays, I don't play sport as much as I'd like but I still take the time to stretch my muscles and tendons.

Stretching keeps your muscles flexible, strong and healthy, and we need that flexibility to maintain a range of motion in the joints. Without it, the muscles shorten and become tight. If this happens, when you need the muscles for activity, they are weak and unable to extend to full motion. That puts you at risk for joint pain, strains, and muscle damage.

There are numerous stretch and yoga workouts you can follow on YouTube. I try to do at least 10 minutes of total body stretching each day and also extra if I have worked a muscle group hard during a workout.

A good tip is to set your alarm 10–15 minutes earlier in the morning. Stretching was the last thing I wanted to do after a long day at work. If you can get into a routine of doing it in the morning it will really set you up for the rest of the day. Also, during the night your movement is very limited, so your muscles shorten. A good stretch in the morning will feel great!

A healthy body equals a healthy mind.

The next pages detail my go-to morning stretch routines.

Stretching routines

7-minute morning stretch routine

Try to hold each stretch for 35 seconds and do 2 rounds.

1) Kneeling hip flexor stretch

Kneel on your right knee, with your toes down. Place your left foot flat on the floor in front of you, your knee should be bent and aligned with your ankle. Place your hands on your left thigh and press your hips forward until you feel tension in the front of your right thigh. Extend your arms overhead, with elbows close to your head and palms facing each other, and slightly arch your back while keeping your chin parallel to the ground.

2) Child's pose

Begin on your hands and knees. Spread your knees wide apart while keeping your big toes touching. Lower your head to the floor and lengthen your spine. Keep your arms extended, palms facing down. Breathe deeply in this position.

3) Doorway stretch

Stand in a doorway and place both arms against each side of the door frame. Your elbow should be aligned with your shoulder. Place your palms on the doorway and slowly lean forward, relax your shoulders and you will feel a great stretch in your chest and shoulder muscles.

4) Pigeon

Start in a press-up position. Bring your right knee between your hands, placing your right ankle near your left wrist. Extend your left leg behind you so your kneecap and the top of your foot rest on the floor. Press through your fingertips as you lift your torso away from your thigh. Lengthen the front of your body and push your bum down to the floor. You will feel a great stretch for the hip flexors and glutes. A must-do especially if you work at a desk all day.

5) Dead Hang

Use a secure overhead bar. Grip the bar with an overhand grip (palms facing away from you). Move your feet off the step or bench so you're hanging onto the bar. Keep your arms straight and dangle for 35 seconds. You may hear your spine pop in the position. Don't worry this is a good thing as you are relieving built-up pressure in your spine.

If you can't dead hang for 35 seconds due to grip strength or access to a bar. Lie with your back and legs on the floor and your arms extended over your head, reach as far as you can with your hands you will feel a great stretch in your core.

6) Assisted hamstring stretch

Lie on the floor with your legs extended in front of you. Loop a band or towel around the ball of one foot. Raise your leg by pulling the towel or band towards you while keeping the knee straight. Keep the other leg flat on the floor.

Repeat (stretch the other side if applicable)

12-minute morning stretch routine

Try to hold each stretch for 30 seconds and do one round:

1) Sky reach and toe touch

With your feet shoulder-width apart, raise your arms to try and touch the ceiling. After a short pause, keep your legs straight and roll your torso forward and try to touch the floor with your hands, pause and then repeat until the 30 seconds are up.

2) Neck roll

Bring your left ear to your left shoulder, then roll your chin down towards the chest, across the chest and up the other side. Continue to circle your neck clockwise for 15 seconds and then repeat anti-clockwise for 15 seconds.

3) Triceps

Extend your right arm to the ceiling, then bend at the elbow to bring the right palm towards the centre of your back, resting your middle finger along your spine. Use your left hand to gently push your elbow in toward the centre and down. Hold for 30 seconds and then repeat on the other side.

4) Shoulders

Reach one arm across your body, using your other arm to hold it gently by your upper arm. Slowly begin to pull your arm toward your chest, as far as possible, allowing the stretch to reach deep into the back of your shoulder.

Hold for 30 seconds and then repeat on the other side.

5) Chest

Bring your hands together behind your back and interlock your fingers. Breathe in deeply to expand your chest and extend your arms as far as possible.

6) Quads

Stand on your left leg, one knee touching the other. You can hold a chair or the wall to keep you steady if needed. Grab your right foot, using your right hand, and pull it towards your bum. Hold for 30 seconds and then repeat on the other side.

7) Calves

Stand near a wall with one foot in front of the other, front knee slightly bent. Keep your back knee straight, your heel on the ground, and lean toward the wall. Feel the stretch all along the calf of your back leg. Hold for 30 seconds and then repeat on the other side.

8) Forward bend

With your feet greater than shoulder-width apart and your legs straight, bend your torso and try to touch your left foot with both hands. Pause briefly and then touch your right foot and repeat for the full 30 seconds.

9) Hip Flexors

Kneel on your right knee, with your toes down. Place your

left foot flat on the floor in front of you, your knee should be bent and aligned with your ankle. Place your hands on your left thigh and press your hips forward until you feel tension in the front of your right thigh. Extend your arms overhead, with elbows close to your head and palms facing each other, and slightly arch your back while keeping your chin parallel to the ground. Hold for 30 seconds and then repeat on the other side.

10) Cat and cow

With your knees and hands on the floor, inhale, arch your back and tilt your head back so you face forward, pause for 2 seconds. Then tuck your chin to your chest and round your back so it is arched whilst exhaling. Hold for 2 seconds and continue to repeat both stretches for 30 seconds.

11) Abs

In a press-up position lower your hips towards the floor. Keep your torso high and look up. Hold for 10 seconds. In the same position tilt your head so you look at your left foot. Hold for 10 seconds. Repeat on the right side to finish the stretch.

12) Hamstrings

Whilst standing, lift your right leg and place it on an elevated surface like your mattress and keep your leg straight, bend forward and with both hands try to touch your right toes. Hold for 30 seconds and then repeat on the other side.

13) Butterfly

Sit up straight and tall with your knees bent. Bring the soles of your feet together, knees opening out to the sides. Grasp your feet and ankles and slowly lean forward, keeping your spine straight. Place your elbows on the tops of your thighs and gently press down until you feel a stretch.

14) Seated Body Twist

Place your right foot flat on the ground next to your left knee. Place your left elbow on the outside of your bent knee, gently pushing your leg inward. Put your right hand on the ground behind your body for stability and gently twist your torso to the right. Hold for 30 seconds and then repeat on the other side.

15) Knee to chest

Lie on your back with your knees bent and your feet flat on the floor. Bring one knee to your chest, keeping the other foot flat on the floor (or the other leg straight, whichever feels better on your lower back). You should feel quite an intense stretch in your glute. Hold for 30 seconds and then repeat on the other side.

16) Happy baby

Staying on the floor, open your knees slightly wider than your torso, then bring them up toward your armpits. Position each ankle directly over the knee, so your shins are perpendicular to the floor. Flex through the heels. Gently push your feet up into your hands as you pull your hands down to create resistance.

Yoga flow

Below is my go-to yoga flow to lengthen the muscles in my body and create mental clarity and calmness. Breathe deeply throughout this yoga practice taking in 10 inhales and 10 exhales of breath per movement before moving on to the next pose:

Exercise

When you exercise, your body releases, chemicals called endorphins. Endorphins interact with the receptors in your brain that reduce your perception of pain, they also trigger a positive feeling in the body and in turn the mind.

When I exercise, I feel more awake, more alert and healthier. In turn, having an exercise plan helps to add structure to the rest of your life. When I exercise, I normally eat better too.

Due to working upwards of 50 hours a week at an old job, I decided not to go to the gym and instead do workouts from home. This saved me loads of time. I was not waiting for equipment; I was straight into a run or bodyweight circuit to get my body moving. The spare bedroom was converted into a mini gym/clothes drying room with the following equipment: pull-up bar, dip bar, a weighted vest, light dumbbells and bands to also add resistance if needed.

My workouts are currently around 20–30 minutes of intense bodyweight or lightweight exercises 5 times a week. Some of my favourite workouts can be found on the upcoming pages. These workouts can be done by anyone. If you are new to working out, please take your time and build up to the full workouts (instead of doing three full rounds just do one round). If you can't do a full press-up do a press-up on your knees. If you are experienced, you might want to add a weighted vest for resistance.

A good tip for my circuit workouts would be to download an interval timer app on your phone and set the low intensity to 5 seconds which will be your transfer time to change onto the next exercise. Use the high-intensity timer for the exercises in the circuit if they are indeed time-related.

If you want to create your own workout plan, you can copy the workout code (UW1, LW1, FW1, AW1) and write it in the DIY workout tables (page 71). I would recommend 5 workouts a week, picking either 2 upper, 2 lower and 1 full-body or 1 upper, 1 lower and 3 full-body workouts from the following pages to create a 3-week plan. Then when the 3 weeks are up, change up your plan by having different workouts to keep your muscles guessing to avoid a training plateau and also, so you don't get bored!

Remember to warm up and get your body loose before going into the full workouts:

30 seconds jumping jacks.
30 seconds arm rotations clockwise.
30 seconds skipping with an imaginary rope.
30 seconds arm rotations anti-clockwise.
30 seconds running butt kicks.
30 seconds high knees running on the spot.

You're ready. No pain, no gain!

Workouts

Upper body workouts (UW)

Full upper body circuit (UW1)

4 rounds, 2-minute rest after each round:

1. 20 press-ups.
2. 20 bent-over reverse flys.
3. 20 dumbbell shoulder presses.
4. 20 bicep curls.
5. 20 dips or overhead tricep extensions.

AMRAP upper body (UW2)

4 rounds of 60-second intervals. As many reps as possible:

1. Press-ups.
2. Rest.
3. Pull-ups (any variation, wide grip is the hardest).
4. Rest.
5. Dips.
6. Rest.

Volume training (UW3)

10 rounds, 1-minute rest after each round:

1. 5–10 pull-ups.
2. 12 press-ups.

Chest burner (UW4)

3 rounds, 2-minute rest after each round:

1. 10 press-ups followed by 10 shoulder taps on each side.
2. 9 press-ups followed by 9 shoulder taps on each side.
3. 8 press-ups followed by 8 shoulder taps on each side.
4. 7 press-ups followed by 7 shoulder taps on each side.
5. 6 press-ups followed by 6 shoulder taps on each side.
6. 5 press-ups followed by 5 shoulder taps on each side.
7. 4 press-ups followed by 4 shoulder taps on each side.
8. 3 press-ups followed by 3 shoulder taps on each side.
9. 2 press-ups followed by 2 shoulder taps on each side.
10. 1 press-up followed by 1 shoulder tap on each side.

Shoulder burner (UW5)

4 rounds, 2-minute rest after each round:

1. 20 dumbbell shoulder presses.
2. 20 dumbbell lateral raises.
3. 20 dumbbell front raises.
4. 20 dumbbell upright rows.
5. 20 dumbbell shrugs.

Countdown arms burner (UW6)

1 round, 1-minute rest between sets:

1. 10 chin-ups followed by 10 dips.
2. 9 chin-ups followed by 9 dips.
3. 8 chin-ups followed by 8 dips.
4. 7 chin-ups followed by 7 dips.
5. 6 chin-ups followed by 6 dips.
6. 5 chin-ups followed by 5 dips.
7. 4 chin-ups followed by 4 dips.
8. 3 chin-ups followed by 3 dips.
9. 2 chin-ups followed by 2 dips.
10. 1 chin-up followed by 1 dip.

The play your cards right chest workout (UW7)

Take a 52-card deck and shuffle the cards so you have no idea which card will come up next. Flip the first card and do however many press-ups the card says. For face cards—jack, queen, and king—do 10 press-ups. When you turn an ace, do 11 press-ups. Once you have made your way through the entire deck you will have done 380 press-ups. Aim to complete the full deck as quick as you can.

*This can also be done with other exercises. I would recommend either squats or lunges for a great leg workout.

Push workout (UW8)

1-minute rest between sets. Rest as necessary during the set to get the reps done:

1. 25 dips.
2. 20 dips.
3. 15 dips.
4. 10 dips.
5. 5 dips.
6. 25 hand-release press-ups.
7. 20 hand-release press-ups.
8. 15 hand-release press-ups.
9. 10 hand-release press-ups.
10. 5 hand-release press-ups.

Press-up matrix (UW9)

1. 10 elbows in press-ups.
2. 10 wide press-ups.
3. 10 palms facing away press-ups.
4. 10 knuckle press-ups.
5. 10 diamond press-ups.
6. Rest 1 minute.
7. Repeat as follows: 2nd set, 7 reps of each; 3rd set, 5 reps; 4th set, 3 reps.

Upper body hypertrophy (UW10)

Complete 3 sets of each exercise before moving on to the
next, with a 1-minute rest between sets:

1. 12 wide grip pull-ups.
2. 12 narrow grip pull-ups.
3. 12 chin-ups.
4. 12 seated rows using a band.
5. 12 incline press-ups.
6. 12 decline press-ups.
7. 12 press-ups.
8. 12 dips.

Lower body workouts (LW)

Leg burner (LW1)

3 rounds, 2-minute rest after each round:

1. 10 squats followed by 20 walking lunges.
2. 9 squats followed by 18 walking lunges.
3. 8 squats followed by 16 walking lunges.
4. 7 squats followed by 14 walking lunges.
5. 6 squats followed by 12 walking lunges.
6. 5 squats followed by 10 walking lunges.
7. 4 squats followed by 8 walking lunges.
8. 3 squats followed by 6 walking lunges.
9. 2 squats followed by 4 walking lunges.
10. 1 squat followed by 2 walking lunges.

Lower body and abs circuit (LW2)

4 rounds, 2-minute rest after each round:

1. 30 squats.
2. 15 Bulgarian split squats (right leg).
3. 15 Bulgarian split squats (left leg).
4. 30 calf raises on the edge of a step.
5. 30 leg raises.
6. 30 Russian twists with weight.

Parker squats (LW3)

3 rounds, 2-minute rest after each round:

Have 10 washing-line pegs laid out in a line roughly 3 inches (around 8cm) apart.

1. Squat down and once your hips and knees are in line reach for the first peg and pick it up and return to standing.
2. Squat down and put the peg in your hand on top of the second peg and stand back up.
3. Squat down and pick one peg up from the pile, squat again and pick the other peg up leaving none and return to standing.
4. Squat down and put both pegs on the next pile.
5. Squat 3 times and pick the 3 pegs up separately on the 4th squat put all pegs on the 4th pile.
6. Repeat all the way to the last pile so you will have to squat down 10 times to pick up all the pegs. Once all the pegs are in your hands that is 1 round complete.

Plyometric leg workout (LW4)

3 rounds, 2-minute rest after each round:

1. 50 squat jumps.
2. 50 jumping lunges.
3. 50 right leg hops.
4. 50 left leg hops.

Legs and core supersets (LW5)

Complete 3 sets of each superset before moving on to the next, with a 1-minute rest between sets:

1a. 20 bodyweight squats.
1b. Leg lifts to failure.

2a. 15 preacher squats with 5kg dumbbell.
2b. Russian twists to failure.

3a. 10 preacher squats with 10kg weighted vest.
3b. Plank holds to failure.

Glute pump (LW6)

3 rounds, 2-minute rest after each round:

1. 20 banded ankle jumping jacks.
2. 20 lateral band walks (each direction).
3. 20 standing glute kicks (each side).
4. 20 squat-stance banded forward walks.
5. 20 squats with lateral leg lifts (each side).
6. 20 clamshells (each side).
7. 20 hip bridge pulses.
8. 20 fire hydrants (each side).
9. 20 hip bridges with alternating leg extensions.
10. 20 donkey kicks (each side).

Banded glute workout (LW7)

3 rounds, 2-minute rest after each round:

1. 15 lying side leg raises (each side).
2. 15 fire hydrants (each side).
3. 15 crossovers (each side).
4. 15 donkey kicks (each side).
5. 15 clamshells (each side).
6. 10 banded squats.
7. 20 squat pulses.

Glute and lower back workout (LW8)

1-minute rest between sets:

1a. 6x12 right leg sofa bridges.
1b. 6x12 left leg sofa bridges.

2a. 3x20 seated abductions with a band.
2b. 3x20 bridge abductions with a band.

3a. 1-minute left leg bridge hold.
3b. 24 left leg bridges.
3c. 30-second left leg bridge hold.

4a. 1-minute right leg bridge hold.
4b. 24 right leg bridges.
4c. 30-second right leg bridge hold.

5a. 1-minute bridge hold.
5b. 24 bridges.
5c. 30-second bridge hold.

Reverse lunge x burpee challenge (LW9)

20 minutes. 10 sets of 1 minute of work and 1 minute of rest:

1. 1st minute: 22 reverse lunges. When completed do as many burpees as you can in the remaining seconds of the minute.

2. 2nd minute: rest.

Make a note of the number of burpees you do in the set. After completing 10 sets add the numbers of burpees up and try to beat your total score next week.

Park workout (LW10)

1-minute rest between sets unless stated:

1. 10x40-metre sprints with active rest (slowly walk back to the start and set off again).
2. 3x5 broad jumps.
3. 3x5 squat jumps.
4. 3x20 single leg moving hops (10 on each side).
5. 3x24 seconds fast feet.
6. 3x12 burpees.

Full-body workouts (FW)

Bodyweight 300 workout (FW1)

1 round, 300 reps with little to no rest:

1. 25 pull-ups.
2. 25 left leg bridges.
3. 25 right leg bridges.
4. 50 press-ups.
5. 50 squats.
6. 50 leg raises.
7. 25 dumbbell cleans and presses right arm.
8. 25 dumbbell cleans and presses left arm.
9. 25 pull-ups.

Pulls and squats superset (FW2)

Complete 3 sets of each superset before moving on to the next, with a 1-minute rest between sets:

1a. Failure wide grip pull-ups.
1b. 20 bodyweight squats.

2a. Failure neutral grip pull-ups.
2b. 15 preacher squats with 5kg.

3a. Failure chin-ups.
3b. 10 preacher squats with 10kg.

600 rep cardio workout (FW3)

2 rounds of 300 reps with little to no rest during rounds, 2-minute rest after each round:

1. 75 jumping jacks.
2. 25 burpees.
3. 50 leg raises.
4. 75 jumping jacks.
5. 50 sit-ups.
6. 25 burpees.

Legs and shoulders burner (FW4)

Little to no rest:

1. 20 walking lunges followed by 20 shoulder presses.
2. 18 walking lunges followed by 18 shoulder presses.
3. 16 walking lunges followed by 16 shoulder presses.
4. 14 walking lunges followed by 14 shoulder presses.
5. 12 walking lunges followed by 12 shoulder presses.
6. 10 walking lunges followed by 10 shoulder presses.
7. 8 walking lunges followed by 8 shoulder presses.
8. 6 walking lunges followed by 6 shoulder presses.
9. 4 walking lunges followed by 4 shoulder presses.
10. 2 walking lunges followed by 2 shoulder presses.

Ascending full-body workout (FW5)

4 rounds, 2-minute rest after each round:

1. 10 pull-ups.
2. 20 shoulder presses.
3. 30 press-ups.
4. 40 sit-ups.
5. 50 squats.

21-minute full-body circuit (FW6)

Each set is for 30 seconds followed by a 10-second rest:

1. Jumping jacks.
2. Wall sit.
3. Press-ups.
4. Crunches.
5. Step-ups.
6. Squats.
7. Tricep dips.
8. Plank.
9. High knees running in place.
10. Lunges.
11. Press-ups.
12. Side plank (swap sides after 15 seconds).
13. Repeat twice more.

Full-body cardio and strength (FW7)

1. 7 minutes skipping (changing jumps throughout e.g., single leg, double leg, split leg jumps).
2. 300 squats, 200 press-ups and 100 pull-ups (20 rounds, 1-minute rest between rounds: 15 squats, 10 press-ups and 5 pull-ups).
3. 7 minutes skipping (changing jumps throughout e.g., single leg, double leg, split leg jumps).

Descending full-body workout (FW8)

3 rounds, 2-minute rest after each round:

1. 50 jumping jacks
2. 40 squats
3. 30 press-ups
4. 20 bridges.
5. 10 burpees.
6. 10 pull-ups.

Speed circuit (FW9)

Aim to complete as fast as you can:

1. 50 down-ups (burpee minus jump).
2. 50 squat jumps.
3. 50 press-ups.
4. 100 jumping lunges.
5. 10 get-ups (lie flat on your back and proceed to get up off the floor).

AMRAP full body circuit (FW10)

As many rounds as possible in 25 minutes:

1. 10 squat jumps.
2. 10 press-ups.
3. 10 sit-ups.
4. 10 lunges (each side).
5. 10 planks to press-ups.
6. 10 leg raises.
7. 10 burpees.

Muscle endurance circuit (FW11)

20 minutes:

1. 1 minute press-ups.
2. 1 minute left leg bridge.
3. 1 minute alternate lunges.
4. 3 minutes stair step-ups with weights.
5. 1 minute shoulder press.
6. 1 minute right leg bridge.
7. 1 minute squats.
8. 3 minutes stair step-ups with weights.
9. 1 minute renegade row.
10. 1 minute calf raises.
11. 2 minutes crunches.
12. 2 minutes leg lifts.
13. 1 minute plank shoulder taps.

100 reps per round circuit (FW12)

As many rounds as possible in 20 minutes:

1. 10 Arnold shoulder presses.
2. 10 squats.
3. 10 press-ups.
4. 10 leg raises.
5. 10 pull-ups.
6. 10 calf raises.
7. 10 dips
8. 10 reverse flys.
9. 20 Russian ab twists with weight.

Skip and lift workout (FW13)

1. 3 minutes skipping.
2. 100 shoulder presses (10 sets of 10 with 10 seconds rest in between sets).
3. 3 minutes skipping.
4. 100 lateral raises (10 sets of 10 with 10 seconds rest in between sets).
5. 3 minutes skipping.
6. 100 rear delt flys (10 sets of 10 with 10 seconds rest in between sets).
7. 3 minutes skipping.
8. 100 upright rows (10 sets of 10 with 10 seconds rest in between sets).
9. 3 minutes skipping.
10. 100 weighted crunches (10 sets of 10 with 10 seconds rest in between sets).

A-Z timed workout (FW14)

Rest as required. Try to beat your time every week:

A. 50 jumping jacks.
B. 25 sit-ups.
C. 30 squats.
D. 15 push-ups.
E. 10 burpees.
F. 25 squat jumps.
G. 30 jumping jacks.
H. 15 sit-ups.
I.   1 minute wall sit.
J. 20 burpees.
K. 20 dips.
L. 40 jumping lunges.
M. 1 minute plank hold.
N. 50 jumping jacks.
O. 25 sit-ups.
P. 20 press-ups.
Q. 35 squats.
R. 15 burpees.
S. 15 dips.
T. 1 minute plank hold.
U. 50 sit-ups.
V. 40 high knees.
W. 20 press-ups.
X. 2 minutes wall sit.
Y. 15 sit-ups.
Z. 25 squat jumps.

Timed reverse pyramid workout (FW15)

Rest as required. Try to beat your time every week:

1. 20 squats, 20 press-ups, 20 reverse crunches.
2. 18 squats, 18 press-ups, 18 reverse crunches.
3. 16 squats, 16 press-ups, 16 reverse crunches.
4. 14 squats, 14 press-ups, 14 reverse crunches.
5. 12 squats, 12 press-ups, 12 reverse crunches.
6. 10 squats, 10 press-ups, 10 reverse crunches.
7. 8 squats, 8 press-ups, 8 reverse crunches.
8. 6 squats, 6 press-ups, 6 reverse crunches.
9. 4 squats, 4 press-ups, 4 reverse crunches.
10. 2 squats, 2 press-ups, 2 reverse crunches.

30 seconds on, 30 seconds off (FW16)

Complete 5 sets of each exercise before moving on to the next. 30 seconds of work, followed by 30 seconds of rest:

1. Mountain climbers.
2. Press-ups.
3. Squats.
4. Sit-ups.
5. Plank.
6. Plank get-ups.
7. Burpees.
8. Squat jumps.

Abs workouts (AW)

Partner abs (AW1)

4 rounds, 2-minute rest after each round:

1. 20 partner sit-ups with locked ankles.
2. 20 partner lying leg raises with throw down.
3. 20 partner planks with alternating high fives.
4. 20 partner alternating leg tucks.

Lower abs (AW2)

3 rounds, 2-minute rest after each round:

1. 20 leg scissors.
2. 12 lying leg lifts.
3. 12 v-sits.
4. 12 reverse crunches.
5. 20 seconds leg holds (heels 12 inches [around 30cm] from the ground).

Killer abs (AW3)

4 rounds of 1 minute of work for each exercise followed by a 2-minute rest after each round:

1. Leg raises alternate sides.
2. Dumbbell bicycle pass-through.
3. Reverse crunch to leg raises.
4. Sit-ups with weight drop and pick-up.

Ab ripper (AW4)

1 round rest as needed:

1. 25 in and outs.
2. 25 forward seated bicycles.
3. 25 reverse seated bicycles.
4. 25 frog crunches.
5. 25 wide leg sit-ups.
6. 25 hip rocks and raises.
7. 25 pulse-ups.
8. 25 scissors.
9. 25 roll-up and v-up combos.
10. 25 oblique v-ups (left).
11. 25 oblique v-ups (right).
12. 25 right leg climbs.
13. 25 left leg climbs.
14. 25 Russian twists.

Design your own workout plan

DD/MM/YY - DD/MM/YY	3-week example plan
Monday	UW1
Tuesday	LW1
Wednesday	REST
Thursday	FBW1
Friday	UW2
Saturday	LW2
Sunday	REST

Monday	
Tuesday	
Wednesday	
Thursday	
Friday	
Saturday	
Sunday	

Monday	
Tuesday	
Wednesday	
Thursday	
Friday	
Saturday	
Sunday	

Monday	
Tuesday	
Wednesday	
Thursday	
Friday	
Saturday	
Sunday	

Monday	
Tuesday	
Wednesday	
Thursday	
Friday	
Saturday	
Sunday	

Monday	
Tuesday	
Wednesday	
Thursday	
Friday	
Saturday	
Sunday	

Monday	
Tuesday	
Wednesday	
Thursday	
Friday	
Saturday	
Sunday	

Monday	
Tuesday	
Wednesday	
Thursday	
Friday	
Saturday	
Sunday	

Monday	
Tuesday	
Wednesday	
Thursday	
Friday	
Saturday	
Sunday	

Monday	
Tuesday	
Wednesday	
Thursday	
Friday	
Saturday	
Sunday	

Monday	
Tuesday	
Wednesday	
Thursday	
Friday	
Saturday	
Sunday	

Monday
Tuesday
Wednesday
Thursday
Friday
Saturday
Sunday

Monday
Tuesday
Wednesday
Thursday
Friday
Saturday
Sunday

Monday
Tuesday
Wednesday
Thursday
Friday
Saturday
Sunday

Monday
Tuesday
Wednesday
Thursday
Friday
Saturday
Sunday

Monday	
Tuesday	
Wednesday	
Thursday	
Friday	
Saturday	
Sunday	

Monday	
Tuesday	
Wednesday	
Thursday	
Friday	
Saturday	
Sunday	

Monday	
Tuesday	
Wednesday	
Thursday	
Friday	
Saturday	
Sunday	

Monday	
Tuesday	
Wednesday	
Thursday	
Friday	
Saturday	
Sunday	

Food

Quite simply, what you eat directly affects the structure and function of your brain and, ultimately, your mood. I eat pretty well throughout the week and stick to a nutritious diet whilst trying to cut out processed foods and sugar.

I think balance is the key to everything. Monday to Friday night I make a conscious effort to make sure there is no chocolate, crisps, chips, fizzy drinks, desserts etc in the house. Having this approach means that on the weekend I can enjoy myself (within reason). The takeaway or meal out on a Friday or Saturday night tastes so good knowing you have gone all week earning your weekend treats. I try to stay disciplined year round with my diet, but I think it's important for your well-being to enjoy your food. I also make exceptions for bank holiday's and annual leave. I won't go on a holiday abroad and not have ice cream because it's a Tuesday—life is to be lived after all!

You can also apply this approach to other areas of your life if applicable (drinking alcohol, gambling). I just think it is about being sensible and having a balance that works for you. The Monday to Friday evening rule alongside my workout routines works well for me.

Having a balanced and nutritious diet rich in vitamin D (the higher your vitamin D levels, the more likely you are to feel happy rather than blue) and other vitamins and minerals can help you in several ways. It can reduce the risk of some diseases, including heart disease, diabetes, stroke, some cancers and osteoporosis. It can also reduce high blood pressure, lower high cholesterol, improve your well-being, and improve your ability to fight off illness and recover from injury.

I notice that when I eat good, tasty and nutritious food, my mood improves and I can think clearer. It also gives me an energy boost, so I can make the most out of my day.

If you currently eat a lot of processed foods or have a particularly bad diet, then changing your diet can be very hard, especially if you are not in the right mindset. It might help to start by making small changes rather than changing your whole diet. For example, try two days a week of eating healthy and build this up to eating well Monday to Friday and having Saturdays and Sundays as "treat days" (be careful not to binge on these days). You might not feel better right away, and there might be times when you feel frustrated. But try to keep going! Even making a very small change can make a difference in the long term.

Making these changes and preparing your own food can be quite daunting, however cooking with others can be a lot of fun, unless you're cooking with Gordon Ramsey on Hell's Kitchen! So, try and get your partner, friends and family involved.

I have always been big on my food, my mum jokes that she and my dad named me Michael after Munching Mike... "Mum, I'm 31 years old, leave me alone!" My mum is an amazing cook. I would love to be able to cook like her one day. My go-to meal is a BBQ and everyone is satisfied when they visit "Mike's Big Bites" for a bank holiday BBQ! I felt amazing a couple of years ago when I walked out of Homebase with the Webber grill and I have not looked back since.

The following recipes are some of my personal favourites, these are not your typical healthy-eating recipes but food should be enjoyed. There is no fun in eating plain chicken and brown rice every day—yes, your physical appearance will probably take a turn for the better but mentally it will be draining. You want the best of both worlds to truly live happily, so my advice as an average guy is to enjoy your food, within reason!

Hopefully, there is something for everyone! Try my low-fat beef burgers recipe for a great midweek treat or change up the 5% fat mince to 20% fat for a great, juicy weekend treat. If you're trying to impress someone then the steak with chimichurri sauce won't go amiss.

Remember balance is key. Bon appétit.

Recipes

Bruschetta

Serves 4. Prep time: 10 minutes. Cooking time: 5 minutes.

Ingredients:

8 thick slices of sourdough bread
75ml extra virgin olive oil
1 garlic clove, minced
A small bunch of basil, chopped or 1 teaspoon of oregano
Salt and pepper
350g vine tomatoes, cored, deseeded and chopped

Method:

1) Preheat the grill to a moderately hot temperature.

2) Brush both sides of the slices of sourdough with a little olive oil and arrange on a grilling tray.

3) Grill for 1–2 minutes on each side until lightly toasted.

4) Stir together the remaining olive oil with the garlic and basil.

5) Season the tomatoes with salt and pepper and add to the olive oil, garlic and basil.

6) Spoon the tomatoes onto the sourdough toast and serve immediately.

Bolognese

Serves 3–4. Prep time: 20 minutes. Cooking time: 1 hour 30 minutes.

Ingredients:

4 tablespoons of extra virgin olive oil
450g 5% fat beef or turkey mince
1 large onion (finely chopped)
4 garlic cloves (finely chopped)
100ml red wine
200ml beef stock
1 tin 400g chopped tomatoes
500g tomato passata
2 tablespoons of finely chopped flat-leaf parsley or 1 tablespoon of dried parsley
1 teaspoon of dried oregano
2 tablespoons of Worcestershire sauce
Juice of ½ lemon
½ teaspoon of salt
Ground black pepper to taste
Cooked jacket potatoes or pasta

Method:

1) Heat the oil in a saucepan over low heat.

2) Add the onion and cook slowly until it has softened and becomes translucent.

3) Add the mince and brown gently, breaking the meat up with a fork and stirring constantly.

4) When the meat has lost its raw look, add the chopped garlic.

5) Add the wine, turn up the heat and cook for 5 minutes until the alcohol has evaporated.

6) Stir in the stock, tomatoes and passata.

7) Season with the herbs, Worcestershire sauce, lemon juice and salt.

8) Bring to a boil and cook for 5 minutes, stirring often.

9) Check the seasoning by tasting the sauce, add pepper to taste.

10) Lower the heat and cook the sauce very gently for about 1 hour 20 mins with the lid on. Stir often to prevent the sauce from sticking (slow simmer).

11) Serve hot with pasta or jacket potatoes.

Homemade beef burgers

Makes 4 burgers. Prep time: 15 minutes. Cooking time: 10 minutes.

Ingredients:

450g 5% fat beef mince
1 beef stock cube
1 tablespoon onion granules
2 tablespoons water
1–2 tablespoons sunflower or olive oil
4 Monterey jack cheese slices
4 brioche burger buns
Tomato slices
Lettuce leaves
Mayonnaise

Method:

1) Place the beef in a large mixing bowl.

2) Crumble the stock cube over the meat, add the onion granules and water and mix well.

3) Divide the meat into portions.

4) Shape the meat into a ball and then flatten slightly to make a patty of your preferred thickness. You can also use a burger press if you have one.

5) Place a griddle pan over medium heat or set up the BBQ coals ready to cook directly over them.

6) Lightly brush the burgers with oil and cook the burgers for 4 minutes.

7) Flip the burgers and add the cheese to let it melt.

8) Cook the burgers for a further 4 minutes.

9) Remove the patties from the pan and let them rest on a plate.

10) Toast the brioche buns

11) Once toasted, apply the mayonnaise and place the lettuce leaves and tomato slices on the bottom half of the bun. Stack your burger and serve.

Turkey burgers

Makes 4 burgers. Prep time: 15 minutes. Cooking time: 10 minutes.

Ingredients:

450g turkey thigh mince
4 tablespoons fresh wholemeal breadcrumbs
1 small onion, finely chopped
1 eating apple, peeled, cored and finely chopped
Grated rind and juice of a small lemon
2 tablespoons finely chopped fresh parsley
1 tablespoon sunflower oil
Salt and pepper
4 burger buns

Method:

1) Places the meat in a large mixing bowl.

2) Add the breadcrumbs, chopped onion, apple, lemon rind, lemon juice and parsley, and mix gently to combine.

3) Divide the meat into 4 portions and shape each one into a burger patty.

4) Preheat a griddle pan on medium-high heat.

5) Brush the patties with the oil and place them onto the preheated frying pan. Cook for 3 minutes on

each side. If there are any traces of pink meat after 6 minutes continue to cook until done.

6) Remove the patties from the pan and set them to one side

7) Toast the burger buns (both sides) on the griddle.

8) Place the burger on the bun base and serve.

Pulled pork

Serves 4–6 Prep time: 10 minutes. Cooking time: 6 hours.

Ingredients:

1.5 kg pork shoulder
250ml apple juice
Salt and pepper

Method:

1) Preheat the oven to 130°C.

2) Season the meat by rubbing salt and pepper over all the non-fatty sides of the shoulder.

3) Use a knife and pierce the fat numerous times.

4) Place the shoulder into an ovenproof dish.

5) Pour 350ml of apple juice onto the fat and allow it to run down to the bottom of the dish.

6) Place a lid on the dish.

7) Cook in the oven on the middle shelf for 6 hours till tender. Keep checking the meat every 1–2 hours. If the dish looks dry top up with apple juice.

8) Shred the meat with two forks.

9) Serve with nachos, in sandwiches, burritos etc.

Pulled pork burritos

Serves 4. Prep time: 15–20 minutes. Cooking time: 20–25 minutes.

Ingredients:

Pulled pork
2 tablespoons sunflower oil
1 onion, finely chopped
3 garlic cloves, minced
Salt and pepper
1 teaspoon ground cumin
A pinch of ground cinnamon
A pinch of cayenne pepper
100ml tomato ketchup
100ml cider vinegar
2 tablespoons soft dark brown sugar
450ml chicken stock
800g cooked pulled pork
75g BBQ sauce
4 large tortillas
100g Monterey jack cheese, grated
1 avocado, pitted and sliced

Salsa
200g canned chopped tomatoes
A pinch of caster sugar
2 tablespoons distilled vinegar
1 garlic clove, minced
A small bunch of coriander, finely chopped

Method:

1) For the pulled pork: Heat the sunflower oil in a large casserole dish set over moderate heat until hot.

2) Add the onion, garlic, salt and pepper and cook until the onion is golden.

3) Add the cumin and cinnamon. Stir well and cook for a further minute.

4) Add the tomato ketchup, cider vinegar, brown sugar and chicken stock.

5) Bring to a simmer, stirring well and often.

6) Add the pork and cook at a gentle simmer for 15–20 minutes.

7) Shred the pork between 2 forks.

8) Add the BBQ sauce and salt and pepper to taste.

9) For the salsa: In a small bowl mix together the chopped tomatoes, caster sugar, distilled vinegar, garlic and the finely chopped coriander.

10) Pile the pulled pork, grated cheese, avocado and prepared salsa onto the centre of the tortillas.

11) Fold, roll and serve as burritos.

Chicken fajitas

Serves 4. Prep time: 15 minutes. Cooking time: 15 minutes.

Ingredients:

3 tablespoons sunflower oil
1 large onion, finely sliced
2 garlic cloves, finely chopped
2 large skinless chicken breasts, sliced into mini fillets
2 teaspoons ground cumin
1 tablespoon smoked paprika
½ teaspoon of chilli powder
A pinch of caster sugar
Salt and pepper
2 avocados, pitted and chopped
1 lime, juiced
4 large tortillas
1 red pepper, finely diced
75g cheese (red Leicester is recommended), grated

Method:

1) Heat the sunflower oil in a large frying pan over moderate heat.

2) Once the oil is hot, add the onion and garlic to the pan and fry for 3–4 minutes.

3) Add the chicken and continue to fry until the chicken is brown all over and cooked through. Sprinkle over the cumin, paprika, chilli powder and caster sugar.

4) Cook for a further minute on reduced heat. Stirring well and often. Add extra salt and pepper at this point to your taste.

5) Take the chicken off the heat and set the frying pan to one side.

6) Mash together the avocado with the lime juice and pepper until smooth.

7) Spread the avocado over the centre of the tortillas, then top with the chicken.

8) Add the red pepper and cheese, fold and serve.

Jerk chicken

Serves 4. Prep time: 20 minutes. Cooking time: 25–30 minutes.

Ingredients:

4 small chicken breasts
3 tablespoons sunflower oil
2 tablespoons jerk spice mix
½ small butternut squash, peeled and chopped into cubes
250g cooked basmati rice
400g canned black beans, drained
675ml chicken stock
Salt and pepper

Method:

1) Preheat the oven to 190°C and line a baking tray with tin foil.

2) Rub the chicken breasts with 2 tablespoons of oil then sprinkle with the jerk mix and place on the baking tray and bake for 25 minutes.

3) While the chicken is in the oven, heat the remaining oil in a large saucepan set over medium heat until hot.

4) Add the butternut squash and the cooked basmati rice. Continue to cook for 2 minutes stirring occasionally.

5) Stir in the black beans and chicken stock and bring to a boil.

6) Cover the saucepan with a lid and continue to cook over reduced heat for 15–20 minutes until the rice and beans become tender.

7) Remove the rice from the heat but keep it covered until your chicken is ready.

8) Remove the chicken and leave it to rest for a couple of minutes.

9) Fluff the rice with a fork and season with salt and pepper.

10) Spoon the rice into bowls and top with the chicken.

Steak with chimichurri sauce

Serves 4. Prep time: 20 minutes. Cooking time: 45–50 minutes.

Ingredients:

450g new potatoes
3 tablespoons olive oil
Flakes of salt and ground pepper
3 tablespoons of red wine vinegar
1 onion, finely chopped
2 red chillies, deseeded and finely chopped
3 garlic cloves, minced
A small bunch of coriander, finely chopped
A small handful of oregano, finely chopped
150ml extra virgin olive oil
4 300g sirloin steaks
2 tablespoons groundnut oil
1 tablespoon unsalted butter
150g asparagus spears, with the ends removed

Method:

1) Arrange the potatoes on a roasting tray and drizzle with 1 tablespoon of olive oil. Then season with salt and pepper.

2) Roast the potatoes for 45–50 minutes until soft on the inside and crisp on the outside.

3) Prepare the chimichurri by stirring together the red wine vinegar, onion, chillies, garlic, coriander and

oregano. Season with salt and pepper to taste and set to one side.

4) 15 minutes before the potatoes are ready, heat a cast-iron frying pan over high heat until hot.

5) Rub the steaks with groundnut oil and season with salt and pepper.

6) Sear the steaks for 2 minutes, turn, add the butter and cook for another 2 minutes (medium-rare) whilst basting with the juices, oil and melted butter. Once done wrap loosely in foil and allow the steaks to rest.

7) Add the asparagus to the pan and cook gently for 5 minutes.

8) Remove the asparagus and potatoes when ready.

9) Slice the steaks and serve with potatoes, asparagus and small cups of chimichurri sauce on the side.

Chilli con carne

Serves 4. Prep time: 5 minutes. Cooking time: 50 minutes.

Ingredients:

450g 5% fat beef or turkey thigh mince
1 can chopped tomatoes
1 can five beans in tomato sauce
1 tablespoon chilli powder
1 teaspoon ground cumin
¼ teaspoon cayenne pepper
¼ teaspoon garlic powder
½ teaspoon onion powder
1 teaspoon salt
¼ teaspoon approximately freshly ground pepper
2 tablespoons sunflower oil

Method:

1) Heat the oil in a saucepan over low heat.

2) Add the mince and brown one side gently

3) Mix the chilli powder, ground cumin, cayenne pepper, garlic powder, onion powder, salt and pepper in a bowl.

4) Turn the mince and start to break it up with the stirring spoon.

5) Add the bowl of herbs and spices.

6) When the meat appears cooked, add the beans and chopped tomatoes.

7) Simmer for 40 minutes with the lid on, stirring occasionally.

8) Serve with rice or jacket potatoes.

Chicken rice box

Serves 5. Prep time: 20 minutes. Cooking time: 25–30 minutes.

Ingredients:

4 chicken breasts
4 handfuls of spinach leaves
1 tablespoon sunflower oil
2 garlic cloves, minced
1 onion, diced
360g uncooked basmati rice
350ml vegetable broth
1 sweetcorn (cooked)
8 tablespoons diced carrots
8 tablespoons frozen peas
¼ teaspoon chilli powder
¼ teaspoon cumin
Salt and pepper, to taste
2 tomatoes, diced

Method:

1) Preheat the oven to 180°C

2) Season the chicken breasts with pepper and wrap in foil. Cook in the oven for 18–20 minutes.

3) Heat the sunflower oil in a large frying pan over medium heat.

4) Add the garlic and onion, stirring frequently for around 2 minutes until the onions have become translucent.

5) Add the rice and stir for about 2 minutes.

6) Stir in the tomatoes and vegetable broth, and bring to a simmer.

7) Stir in the carrots, peas, chilli powder and cumin. Season with salt and pepper, to taste.

8) Bring to a boil, cover the pan and reduce the heat and simmer until the rice is cooked through which should take roughly 15 minutes.

9) Stir in the diced tomatoes.

10) Cut the chicken into small chunks and cut the corn from the cob and stir both into the rice.

11) Serve into takeaway tubs leaving a third of the tub free.

12) Add the spinach and enjoy it as a tasty evening meal or for your lunches for the majority of the week.

Chicken donor kebab

Serves 4. Prep time: 15 minutes. Cooking time: 60 minutes.

Ingredients:

5 chicken breasts (sliced in half)
500ml Greek natural yoghurt
1 tablespoon olive oil
1 tablespoon smoked paprika
1 tablespoon cumin
1 tablespoon chilli powder
1 tablespoon salt
1 teaspoon turmeric
1 teaspoon garam masala
Juice of ½ a lemon
½ lemon
½ onion
Lettuce, as required
4 pitta bread

Method:

1) Place the chicken, yoghurt, oil, lemon juice, salt and spices into a mixing bowl and stir the ingredients together.

2) Skewer through the half onion (flat side facing down as the stand).

3) Layer the chicken breasts through the skewer to create the kebab.

4) Add the half lemon to the top of the skewer.

5) If needed add a second or a third skewer for balance.

6) Place on a baking tray and cook for 60 minutes at 180°C.

7) Serve with lettuce and pitta bread.

Chicken karahi

Serves 2. Prep time: 15 minutes. Cooking time: 40 minutes.

Ingredients:

600g diced chicken
1 onion finely chopped
60ml ginger (finely diced) or ½ teaspoon ground ginger
2 tablespoons garlic (minced)
1 can chopped tomatoes
1 teaspoon ground cumin
1 teaspoon ground coriander
1 teaspoon garam masala
1 tablespoon Kashmiri red chilli powder
¼ teaspoon ground turmeric
1.5 teaspoons kosher salt
2 tablespoons olive oil

Method:

1) Add the olive oil to a large frying pan and bring it to medium heat.

2) Add the onions, ginger and garlic and cook for 3 minutes.

3) Add the chicken, chopped tomatoes, ground cumin, ground coriander, garam masala, Kashmiri red chilli powder, ground turmeric and salt. Stir well.

4) Cover the pan and leave to cook for 20 minutes.

5) Serve with rice.

Yorkshire puddings

Makes 9. Prep: 5 minutes. Cooking time: 30 minutes.

Ingredients:

2 eggs
60g flour
150ml milk
Salt and pepper
Olive oil

Method:

1) In a mixing bowl crack the eggs and add the flour, milk, salt and pepper.

2) Whisk till the batter has no lumps and refrigerate.

3) 1 hour before cooking, take the batter out of the fridge.

4) Preheat a bun tray in the oven (220°C) with a tablespoon of oil in each section.

5) Once the oil is piping hot pour the batter into the bun tray and close the oven door.

6) Cook for 30 minutes without opening the oven door, adjusting the temperature if necessary.

7) Serve with gravy.

BBQ pit beans

Serves 18. Prep time: 15 minutes. Cooking time: 2–3 hours.

Ingredients:

BBQ Sauce
230ml yellow mustard
230ml distilled vinegar
150ml tomato ketchup
105g brown sugar
3 garlic cloves, smashed
½ teaspoon cayenne
½ teaspoon freshly ground pepper
1 tablespoon olive oil

Baked beans
4 cans of baked beans, drained and rinsed thoroughly
500ml pulled pork
1 large onion, diced
3 garlic cloves, minced
85g brown sugar
60ml maple syrup
1 can chopped tomatoes
350ml beef stock
Salt and pepper
2 tablespoons olive oil

Method:

1) To make the BBQ sauce, add 1 tablespoon olive oil to a large saucepan and bring to medium heat.

2) Add the mustard, vinegar, ketchup, brown sugar, smashed garlic, cayenne, and black pepper.

3) Simmer for 10 minutes until the sugar has dissolved, and then remove from the heat.

4) After the BBQ sauce has cooled, remove the smashed garlic cloves from the sauce and discard.

5) Add 2 tablespoons olive oil to a large cooking pan and bring to medium-high heat.

6) Cook the onion for 5 minutes. Sprinkle with salt and pepper, mix in the garlic and cook for 1 more minute.

7) Add the BBQ sauce, pulled pork, sugar, stock, maple syrup, a sprinkle of salt and pepper, beans and chopped tomatoes and bring to a boil.

8) Transfer to a baking dish and place in the oven and bake until thick and fragrant at 180°C for about 2 hours.

9) For best results, smoke on a charcoal-fired BBQ for 1 hour whilst cooking the rest of your food.

Spicy sausage pasta

Serves 4. Prep time: 5 minutes. Cooking time: 1 hour.

Ingredients:

6 caramelised sausages (skin off)
1 onion, finely chopped
1 garlic clove, finely chopped
1 can chopped tomatoes
1 tablespoon tomato puree
1 teaspoon chilli flakes
1 teaspoon oregano
250ml red wine
Salt and pepper
3 tablespoons olive oil
Penne pasta

Method:

1) Add the olive oil to a large saucepan and bring to medium heat.

2) Add the garlic and onion, stirring frequently for around 2 minutes until the onions have become translucent.

3) Add the sausage and tomato puree and stir well to break up the sausage meat.

4) Add the wine and turn up the heat for 2 minutes.

5) Add the chopped tomatoes, oregano, chilli flakes and salt and pepper.

6) Cover the saucepan with a lid and leave to simmer for 50 minutes (stirring occasionally).

7) Serve with cooked penne pasta.

Talking

I recently heard an old Japanese tale about a samurai warrior and his three sons: the samurai wanted to teach his sons about teamwork. He gave each of them one of his arrows and asked them to break the arrows one by one. No problem. Each son did so easily. The samurai then gave them a bundle of three arrows bound together and asked them to repeat the process, none of them could.

The lesson we learn from this tale is that we are stronger together. A problem shared is also a problem halved. One of the most important things you can do to help improve your mental health is one of the most natural things in the world... talk to people.

Don't hold onto things and let them build up, speak to someone about how you are feeling. There is clear evidence that building good relationships with family, friends and your wider community is positive for your well-being. Having strong relationships can help you to share your feelings and know you're being understood. It means you will have support if you are going through a difficult time.

If you do not feel comfortable talking to family or friends, there are a number of mental health helplines such as the Mind charity's info line where you can talk in confidence to one of their knowledgeable team members and get any advice you need.

Talking about your feelings isn't a sign of weakness. It's part of taking charge of your well-being and doing what you can to stay healthy.

Remember, we all have scars and we'll get more. There will be problems and tough times down the road that we have to navigate through. You're not alone. Your mental and physical well-being is paramount for living a healthy life and sometimes when you get knocked down, you will feel like you can't get up. But as the saying goes, "fall down seven times, stand up eight." Choose to never give up hope, talk to people about your feelings, surround yourself with support and make sure you exercise, eat nutritious food, get sunlight, get enough sleep and consume enough positive material.

This brings me back to the reason I started writing this book. I wanted to help someone close to me who had been suffering, by sharing my ideas and what has worked for me. I hope that it can lend a hand to you if you need it. It might teach you something, make you laugh, inspire you, remind you or even help you forget for a few hours! Hopefully, it will give you some tools for your toolbox to use in everyday life.

I'm not the most academic, qualified or healthiest person I know, but I love to help, I care so much, and I'll always be there to lift you off the ground.

Life is for living but make sure you are working hard on yourself.

All the best,

Michael

Three good things daily journal

Use this journal to simply record the good things that have happened each day. "Every day may not be good... but there's something good in every day." No matter how big or small there is always something to be grateful for.

Day	Three good things
Example	1. I made a nice dinner. 2. I listened to my favourite album. 3. I went for a long walk.
Day 1	1. 2. 3.
Day 2	1. 2. 3.
Day 3	1. 2. 3.

Day 4	1.
	2.
	3.
Day 5	1.
	2.
	3.
Day 6	1.
	2.
	3.
Day 7	1.
	2.
	3.
Day 8	1.
	2.
	3.

Day 9	1.
	2.
	3.
Day 10	1.
	2.
	3.
Day 11	1.
	2.
	3.
Day 12	1.
	2.
	3.
Day 13	1.
	2.
	3.

Day 14	1.
	2.
	3.
Day 15	1.
	2.
	3.
Day 16	1.
	2.
	3.
Day 17	1.
	2.
	3.
Day 18	1.
	2.
	3.

Day 19	1.
	2.
	3.
Day 20	1.
	2.
	3.
Day 21	1.
	2.
	3.
Day 22	1.
	2.
	3.
Day 23	1.
	2.
	3.

Day 24	1.
	2.
	3.

Day 25	1.
	2.
	3.

Day 26	1.
	2.
	3.

Day 27	1.
	2.
	3.

Day 28	1.
	2.
	3.

Day 29	1.
	2.
	3.
Day 30	1.
	2.
	3.
Day 31	1.
	2.
	3.
Day 32	1.
	2.
	3.
Day 33	1.
	2.
	3.

Day 34	1. 2. 3.
Day 35	1. 2. 3.
Day 36	1. 2. 3.
Day 37	1. 2. 3.
Day 38	1. 2. 3.

Day 39	1. 2. 3.
Day 40	1. 2. 3.
Day 41	1. 2. 3.
Day 42	1. 2. 3.
Day 43	1. 2. 3.

Day 44	1. 2. 3.
Day 45	1. 2. 3.
Day 46	1. 2. 3.
Day 47	1. 2. 3.
Day 48	1. 2. 3.

Day 49	1. 2. 3.
Day 50	1. 2. 3.
Day 51	1. 2. 3.
Day 52	1. 2. 3.
Day 53	1. 2. 3.

Day 54	1. 2. 3.
Day 55	1. 2. 3.
Day 56	1. 2. 3.
Day 57	1. 2. 3.
Day 58	1. 2. 3.

Day 59	1.
	2.
	3.
Day 60	1.
	2.
	3.
Day 61	1.
	2.
	3.
Day 62	1.
	2.
	3.
Day 63	1.
	2.
	3.

Day 64	1.
	2.
	3.
Day 65	1.
	2.
	3.
Day 66	1.
	2.
	3.
Day 67	1.
	2.
	3.
Day 68	1.
	2.
	3.

Day 69	1. 2. 3.
Day 70	1. 2. 3.
Day 71	1. 2. 3.
Day 72	1. 2. 3.
Day 73	1. 2. 3.

Day 74	1. 2. 3.
Day 75	1. 2. 3.
Day 76	1. 2. 3.
Day 77	1. 2. 3.
Day 78	1. 2. 3.

Day 79	1. 2. 3.
Day 80	1. 2. 3.
Day 81	1. 2. 3.
Day 82	1. 2. 3.
Day 83	1. 2. 3.

Day 84	1.
	2.
	3.
Day 85	1.
	2.
	3.
Day 86	1.
	2.
	3.
Day 87	1.
	2.
	3.
Day 88	1.
	2.
	3.

Day 89	1. 2. 3.
Day 90	1. 2. 3.
Day 91	1. 2. 3.
Day 92	1. 2. 3.
Day 93	1. 2. 3.

Day 94	1.
	2.
	3.
Day 95	1.
	2.
	3.
Day 96	1.
	2.
	3.
Day 97	1.
	2.
	3.
Day 98	1.
	2.
	3.

Day 99	1.
	2.
	3.
Day 100	1.
	2.
	3.
Day 101	1.
	2.
	3.
Day 102	1.
	2.
	3.
Day 103	1.
	2.
	3.

Day 104	1. 2. 3.
Day 105	1. 2. 3.
Day 106	1. 2. 3.
Day 107	1. 2. 3.
Day 108	1. 2. 3.

Day 109	1. 2. 3.
Day 110	1. 2. 3.
Day 111	1. 2. 3.
Day 112	1. 2. 3.
Day 113	1. 2. 3.

Day 114	1. 2. 3.
Day 115	1. 2. 3.
Day 116	1. 2. 3.
Day 117	1. 2. 3.
Day 118	1. 2. 3.

Day 119	1. 2. 3.
Day 120	1. 2. 3.
Day 121	1. 2. 3.
Day 122	1. 2. 3.
Day 123	1. 2. 3.

Day 124	1. 2. 3.
Day 125	1. 2. 3.
Day 126	1. 2. 3.
Day 127	1. 2. 3.
Day 128	1. 2. 3.

Day 129	1. 2. 3.
Day 130	1. 2. 3.
Day 131	1. 2. 3.
Day 132	1. 2. 3.
Day 133	1. 2. 3.

Day 134	1.
	2.
	3.
Day 135	1.
	2.
	3.
Day 136	1.
	2.
	3.
Day 137	1.
	2.
	3.
Day 138	1.
	2.
	3.

Day 139	1. 2. 3.
Day 140	1. 2. 3.
Day 141	1. 2. 3.
Day 142	1. 2. 3.
Day 143	1. 2. 3.

Day 144	1.
	2.
	3.

Day 145	1.
	2.
	3.

Day 146	1.
	2.
	3.

Day 147	1.
	2.
	3.

Day 148	1.
	2.
	3.

Day 149	1. 2. 3.
Day 150	1. 2. 3.
Day 151	1. 2. 3.
Day 152	1. 2. 3.
Day 153	1. 2. 3.

Day 154	1. 2. 3.
Day 155	1. 2. 3.
Day 156	1. 2. 3.
Day 157	1. 2. 3.
Day 158	1. 2. 3.

Day 159	1.
	2.
	3.
Day 160	1.
	2.
	3.
Day 161	1.
	2.
	3.
Day 162	1.
	2.
	3.
Day 163	1.
	2.
	3.

Day 164	1.
	2.
	3.

Day 165	1.
	2.
	3.

Day 166	1.
	2.
	3.

Day 167	1.
	2.
	3.

Day 168	1.
	2.
	3.

Day 169	1. 2. 3.
Day 170	1. 2. 3.
Day 171	1. 2. 3.
Day 172	1. 2. 3.
Day 173	1. 2. 3.

Day 174	1. 2. 3.
Day 175	1. 2. 3.
Day 176	1. 2. 3.
Day 177	1. 2. 3.
Day 178	1. 2. 3.

Day 179	1.
	2.
	3.
Day 180	1.
	2.
	3.
Day 181	1.
	2.
	3.
Day 182	1.
	2.
	3.
Day 183	1.
	2.
	3.

Day 184	1. 2. 3.
Day 185	1. 2. 3.
Day 186	1. 2. 3.
Day 187	1. 2. 3.
Day 188	1. 2. 3.

Day 189	1. 2. 3.
Day 190	1. 2. 3.
Day 191	1. 2. 3.
Day 192	1. 2. 3.
Day 193	1. 2. 3.

Day 194	1. 2. 3.
Day 195	1. 2. 3.
Day 196	1. 2. 3.
Day 197	1. 2. 3.
Day 198	1. 2. 3.

Day 199	1. 2. 3.
Day 200	1. 2. 3.
Day 201	1. 2. 3.
Day 202	1. 2. 3.
Day 203	1. 2. 3.

Day 204	1. 2. 3.
Day 205	1. 2. 3.
Day 206	1. 2. 3.
Day 207	1. 2. 3.
Day 208	1. 2. 3.

Day 209	1. 2. 3.
Day 210	1. 2. 3.
Day 211	1. 2. 3.
Day 212	1. 2. 3.
Day 213	1. 2. 3.

Day 214	1.
	2.
	3.
Day 215	1.
	2.
	3.
Day 216	1.
	2.
	3.
Day 217	1.
	2.
	3.
Day 218	1.
	2.
	3.

Day 219	1.
	2.
	3.
Day 220	1.
	2.
	3.
Day 221	1.
	2.
	3.
Day 222	1.
	2.
	3.
Day 223	1.
	2.
	3.

Day 224	1. 2. 3.
Day 225	1. 2. 3.
Day 226	1. 2. 3.
Day 227	1. 2. 3.
Day 228	1. 2. 3.

Day 229	1. 2. 3.
Day 230	1. 2. 3.
Day 231	1. 2. 3.
Day 232	1. 2. 3.
Day 233	1. 2. 3.

Day 234	1. 2. 3.
Day 235	1. 2. 3.
Day 236	1. 2. 3.
Day 237	1. 2. 3.
Day 238	1. 2. 3.

Day 239	1.
	2.
	3.
Day 240	1.
	2.
	3.
Day 241	1.
	2.
	3.
Day 242	1.
	2.
	3.
Day 243	1.
	2.
	3.

Day 244	1. 2. 3.
Day 245	1. 2. 3.
Day 246	1. 2. 3.
Day 247	1. 2. 3.
Day 248	1. 2. 3.

Day 249	1. 2. 3.
Day 250	1. 2. 3.
Day 251	1. 2. 3.
Day 252	1. 2. 3.
Day 253	1. 2. 3.

Day 254	1. 2. 3.
Day 255	1. 2. 3.
Day 256	1. 2. 3.
Day 257	1. 2. 3.
Day 258	1. 2. 3.

Day 259	1. 2. 3.
Day 260	1. 2. 3.
Day 261	1. 2. 3.
Day 262	1. 2. 3.
Day 263	1. 2. 3.

Day 264	1. 2. 3.
Day 265	1. 2. 3.
Day 266	1. 2. 3.
Day 267	1. 2. 3.
Day 268	1. 2. 3.

Day 269	1. 2. 3.
Day 270	1. 2. 3.
Day 271	1. 2. 3.
Day 272	1. 2. 3.
Day 273	1. 2. 3.

Day 274	1. 2. 3.
Day 275	1. 2. 3.
Day 276	1. 2. 3.
Day 277	1. 2. 3.
Day 278	1. 2. 3.

Day 279	1. 2. 3.
Day 280	1. 2. 3.
Day 281	1. 2. 3.
Day 282	1. 2. 3.
Day 283	1. 2. 3.

Day 284	1. 2. 3.
Day 285	1. 2. 3.
Day 286	1. 2. 3.
Day 287	1. 2. 3.
Day 288	1. 2. 3.

Day 289	1. 2. 3.
Day 290	1. 2. 3.
Day 291	1. 2. 3.
Day 292	1. 2. 3.
Day 293	1. 2. 3.

Day 294	1. 2. 3.
Day 295	1. 2. 3.
Day 296	1. 2. 3.
Day 297	1. 2. 3.
Day 298	1. 2. 3.

Day 299	1. 2. 3.
Day 300	1. 2. 3.
Day 301	1. 2. 3.
Day 302	1. 2. 3.
Day 303	1. 2. 3.

Day 304	1. 2. 3.
Day 305	1. 2. 3.
Day 306	1. 2. 3.
Day 307	1. 2. 3.
Day 308	1. 2. 3.

Day 309	1. 2. 3.
Day 310	1. 2. 3.
Day 311	1. 2. 3.
Day 312	1. 2. 3.
Day 313	1. 2. 3.

Day 314	1. 2. 3.
Day 315	1. 2. 3.
Day 316	1. 2. 3.
Day 317	1. 2. 3.
Day 318	1. 2. 3.

Day 319	1.
	2.
	3.
Day 320	1.
	2.
	3.
Day 321	1.
	2.
	3.
Day 322	1.
	2.
	3.
Day 323	1.
	2.
	3.

Day 324	1. 2. 3.
Day 325	1. 2. 3.
Day 326	1. 2. 3.
Day 327	1. 2. 3.
Day 328	1. 2. 3.

Day 329	1.
	2.
	3.
Day 330	1.
	2.
	3.
Day 331	1.
	2.
	3.
Day 332	1.
	2.
	3.
Day 333	1.
	2.
	3.

Day 334	1. 2. 3.
Day 335	1. 2. 3.
Day 336	1. 2. 3.
Day 337	1. 2. 3.
Day 338	1. 2. 3.

Day 339	1.
	2.
	3.
Day 340	1.
	2.
	3.
Day 341	1.
	2.
	3.
Day 342	1.
	2.
	3.
Day 343	1.
	2.
	3.

Day 344	1. 2. 3.
Day 345	1. 2. 3.
Day 346	1. 2. 3.
Day 347	1. 2. 3.
Day 348	1. 2. 3.

Day 349	1.
	2.
	3.
Day 350	1.
	2.
	3.
Day 351	1.
	2.
	3.
Day 352	1.
	2.
	3.
Day 353	1.
	2.
	3.

Day 354	1. 2. 3.
Day 355	1. 2. 3.
Day 356	1. 2. 3.
Day 357	1. 2. 3.
Day 358	1. 2. 3.

Day 359	1.
	2.
	3.
Day 360	1.
	2.
	3.
Day 361	1.
	2.
	3.
Day 362	1.
	2.
	3.
Day 363	1.
	2.
	3.

Day 364	1. 2. 3.
Day 365	1. 2. 3.

Motivational quotes

"I believe depression is legitimate. But I also believe that if you don't exercise, eat nutritious food, get sunlight, get enough sleep, consume enough positive material, surround yourself with support, then you aren't giving yourself a fighting chance."—Jim Carrey

"Every day may not be good… but there's something good in every day."—Alice Morse Earle

"The happiest people don't have the best of everything they just make the best of everything they have."—Unknown

"Always end the day with a positive thought. No matter how hard things were, tomorrow is a fresh opportunity to make it better."—Unknown

"Train your mind to see the good in everything. Positivity is a choice. The happiness of your life depends on the quality of your thoughts."—Unknown

"Success isn't the key to happiness. Happiness is the key to success."—Albert Schweitzer

"In nature nothing is perfect, and everything is perfect. Trees can be contorted, bent in weird ways and they're still beautiful."—Alice Walker

"20 years ago, the internet was an escape from the real world. Today the real world is an escape from the internet."—Unknown

"A day without laughter is a day wasted."—Charlie Chaplin

"Laughter is the best medicine."—Proverb

"A good laugh heals a lot of hurts."— Madeleine L'Engle

"Always laugh when you can. It is cheap medicine."—Lord Byron

"Live every moment, laugh every day, love beyond words."—Unknown

"Do what makes you happy, be with who makes you smile, laugh as much as you breathe, love as long as you live."— Rachel Ann Nunes

"Live well, laugh often, love much."—Bessie Anderson Stanley

"Happiness can be found, even in the darkest of times, if one only remembers to turn on the light."—J.K. Rowling, *Harry Potter and the Prisoner of Azkaban*

"My dark days made me strong. Or maybe I already was strong, and they made me prove it."—Emery Lord

"The more you praise and celebrate your life, the more there is in life to celebrate."—Oprah Winfrey

"Probably the biggest insight… is that happiness is not just a place but also a process. …Happiness is an ongoing process of fresh challenges, and… it takes the right attitudes and activities to continue to be happy."—Ed Diener

"More smiling, less worrying. More compassion, less judgement. More blessed, less stressed. More love, less hate."—Roy T. Bennett

"Everybody wants happiness, and nobody wants pain, but you can't have a rainbow without a little rain."—Zion Lee

"Of course, mind and body are not separate. So, to be well, cultivate a healthy body and a healthy mind."—Dr Dalton Exley

"Let go of what you can't control. Channel all that energy into living fully in the now."—Karen Salmansohn

"True happiness is… to enjoy the present without anxious dependence upon the future."—Lucius Annaeus Seneca

"The soul always knows what to do to heal itself. The challenge is to silence the mind."—Caroline Myss

"The secret of health for both mind and body is not to mourn for the past, worry about the future, or anticipate troubles, but to live the present moment wisely and earnestly."—Buddha

"Never regret a day in your life: good days give happiness, bad days give experience, worst days give lessons, and best days give memories."—Unknown

"Money is numbers and numbers never end. If it takes money to be happy, your search for happiness will never end."—Bob Marley

"Every strike brings me closer to the next home run."—Babe Ruth

"Two things to remember in life: 'Take care of your thoughts when you're alone,' and 'Take care of your words when you're with people.' "—Zig Ziglar

"Courage is being yourself every day in a world that tells you to be someone else."—Unknown

"Nothing good ever comes from worrying or sitting there feeling sorry for yourself… Keep positive and keep pushing on and things will turn good."—Connor McGregor

"Laugh like you're 10. Party like you're 20. Travel like you're 30. Think like you're 40. Advise like you're 50. Care like you're 60. Love like you're 70."—Unknown

"Be the moon and inspire people even when you're far from full."—K. Tolnoe

"Don't compare your life to others. There's no comparison between the sun and the moon. They shine when it's their time."—Unknown

"If you want to conquer fear, don't sit at home and think about it. Go out and get busy."—Dale Carnegie

"If you stay positive in a negative situation, you win."—Unknown

"An open mind will always open new doors."—Shina Peller

"We don't stop playing because we grow old; we grow old because we stop playing." —George Bernard Shaw

"Reading to the mind is what exercise is to the body."—Joseph Addison

"A negative mind will never give you a positive life."—Ziad K. Abdelnour

"And in the end, it's not the years in your life that count. It's the life in your years."—Edward J. Stieglitz

"When it rains look for rainbows, when it's dark looks for stars."—Unknown

"Darkness cannot drive out darkness: only love can do that. Hate cannot drive out hate: only love can do that."—Martin Luther King Jr.

"Happiness is to be found along the way, not at the end of the road, for then the journey is over and it is too late."—Robert Updegraff

"We cannot direct the wind, but we can adjust the sails."—Unknown

"Have a go, what's the worst that could happen?"—Unknown

About the author

Printed in Great Britain
by Amazon

87278595R00119